CATS

KINGFISHER BOOKS
WARD LOCK LIMITED

First published in 1981 by Kingfisher Books Limited
47 Marylebone Lane, London W1M 6AX

Colour separations by Newsele Litho Ltd, Milan, London
Printed and bound in Italy by Vallardi Industrie
Grafiche, Milan

BRITISH LIBRARY CATALOGUING
IN PUBLICATION DATA
  Loxton, Howard
  Cats (Kingfisher guides)
  1. Cats
  I. Title   II. Series
  636.8   SF442

ISBN 0-7063-6101-6

AUTHOR
HOWARD LOXTON

DESIGNED AND EDITED
BY
KEITH LYE

ILLUSTRATED
BY
David Nockels   Joan Thomson
John Thompson   Roy Wiltshire

CONSULTANT
ELIZABETH TOWE

CONTENTS

Introduction	. 8	Short-Haired Cats	. 46
Anatomy and Senses	. 10	Long-Haired Cats	. 72
The Story of the Cat	. 24	Foreign Short-Hairs	. 98
The Development of		Glossary	. 122
Breeds	. 35	Index	. 124

INTRODUCTION

A familiar cat sleeping, curled up in the living room, is a symbol of the home, of security and of peaceful domesticity. However, when the cat awakes, stretches its limbs, opens its eyes, yawns and shows its teeth, it changes into a symbol of the wild. Its tabby stripes become the marking of the tiger. Its eyes flash with predatory fire. Its paws unsheath their sharp and slashing claws and its teeth are the ravening fangs of the carnivore. Both images are true. The cat can be the most gentle and home-loving of pets, but it is also the cousin of the lion and tiger. Today, the cat is, perhaps, the most familiar of all our domestic animals. Its domesticity, however, is very recent, compared with such creatures as dogs, asses, goats and farmyard cattle. This explains why our domestic pet differs so little from a wild cat.

The cat shares a common ancestor with the dog, weasel and other small mammals. This was a long-bodied, short-legged carnivore, which looked rather weasel-like. Palaeontologists have named it *Miacis* and it lived about 50 million years ago. Over the following 10 million years, one branch of its descendants evolved into a truly cat-like animal. This creature was named *Dinictis*. It was about the same size as a modern lynx and looked much like the big cats of today, except that it had very big canine teeth. Its brain, however, was small. One branch of descendants from *Dinictis* developed even larger canine teeth. This branch produced the now extinct sabre-toothed tiger of the Pleistocene epoch. Some

Smilodon (*a prehistoric sabre-toothed tiger*), the modern tiger, the cheetah, the puma and the domestic cat are all members of the same family.

Smilodon

Tiger

scientists consider that *Dinictis* itself belongs with the sabre-toothed tigers and that there may be an as yet unidentified common ancestor of both the sabre-toothed tigers and the other branch which became the Felidae, the name for the family to which all living cats belong.

Modern cats range from the Siberian Tiger, which may measure nearly 4 metres (over 13 ft) from nose to tail tip, to the Rusty-spotted Cat of India and Sri Lanka, which is only 60 cm (2 ft) long. There are 36 species of cats in all. They include the Lion, the Leopard, the Cheetah, the Puma, the Lynx, the Bobcat, the Jaguar and the Ocelot, the Serval, the Caracal, the Jaguarondi and the Margay, as well as various smaller cats which are native in different parts of the world. Several of the small cats may have played a part in the development of the domestic cat. However, experts generally agree that the domestic cat's closest relations are the African Wild Cat (*Felis libyca*) and the European Wild Cat (*Felis silvestris*). The domestic cat can breed with them and feral animals may revert to the coat pattern and type of the wild cats after a few generations.

The domestication of the cat is so recent, comparatively, that it has had only a superficial effect on the animal's physique and nature. Cats have learned to make the most of the homes and facilities that their owners provide. They show affection and sometimes, it seems, a genuine concern for people close to them. Whether through imprinting, through a retarded adolescent state produced by domestication, or through some more conscious process, many domestic cats seem to want to share the lives of their owners. This, however, is only the veneer of domestication. Wild animals of many kinds have developed a closeness to and a rapport with humans. The physique and instincts of the domestic pet are still those of the wild cat. Its senses and skills are those of the predator. This fact is evident to anyone who has watched a cat about its daily business.

Puma

Cheetah

Domestic cat

ANATOMY AND SENSES

The most noticeable differences between the skeletons of a cat and a person are the tail, which has disappeared in man, and the fact that the cat carries its weight upon its paws. The equivalent of the paws is the part of our skeleton which forms the fingers, the 'knuckle' being what seems to be their heel, and the equivalent of our heel being the first joint up their legs. There are many other differences. For example, the cat's spine is much more pliable than ours, enabling it to arch its back, and its limbs are extremely flexible. The head can be turned much more to the rear than ours.

The skeleton is linked by extremely powerful muscles. These are particularly strong in the area of the pelvis and the rear legs, so that the cat can make prodigious leaps. Muscles in the neck and shoulders are used in striking prey.

The cat is a hunter in the wild. It depends for food largely on the prey it kills and so its digestive system has to be adapted to coping with occasional large meals and, sometimes, longish periods without any food. To do this its stomach and intestines must be large and take up more space than ours, proportionally. In consequence the rib cage is proportionally smaller and the space available to accomodate the lungs and heart is restricted. This means that although a cat can produce bursts of

The cat's skeleton has a similar appearance to our own, plus a tail, but many of the bones, such as the pelvis, are very different in shape.

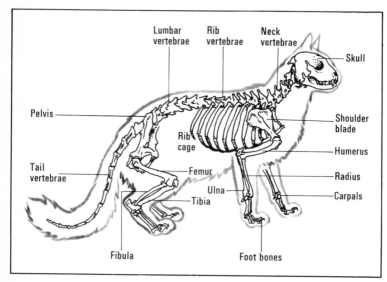

A cat can leap to considerable heights and across wide spaces. It judges distances with great accuracy.

great speed and energy, it cannot sustain violent activity for long and must pause to recover from the strain. Even when at rest, a cat breathes in and out more than twice as often as we do in the same period.

The part of the cat's brain which controls its powerful muscles and flexible limbs is particularly well-developed and it is linked to them by a finely tuned nervous and sensory system. The cat's sense organs respond to a wide range and fine variation of stimuli. They enable it to observe and react to a degree which, generally, far surpasses our own. Only the sense of taste is relatively undeveloped. This is not of great importance to the cat in hunting prey or eluding enemies, the purposes for which its sensory equipment and fine physique have evolved.

Sight

Cats locate prey by sight and sound and so both their eyes and ears are particularly sensitive. Their perception of colour, however, is limited and they have only about one-sixth of the proportion of colour-recording elements in the eye that we have. Our perception of colour no doubt helps us to separate shapes, while cats seem less able to distinguish stationary objects from their background. In addition, their eyes do not focus on very close objects. Like us, cats have eyes that are placed so that both can look in the same direction. This gives them stereoscopic vision, which enables them to judge distances. From the accuracy with which they can leap, it is clear that their spatial judgement and matched physical control is considerable. Each eye has an angle of vision of nearly 205° and, coupled with their extremely flexible necks, cats get a wide field of vision with a minimum of movement.

11

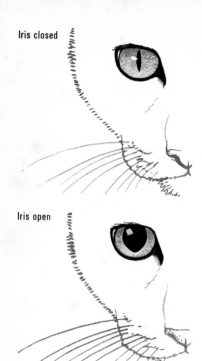

Iris closed

Iris open

Nictitating membrane

The iris of the cat's eye can close to a narrow slit or open to a full circle. This controls the amount of light which enters the eye, enabling cats to make maximum use of the minimum amount of light so that they can 'see in the dark'. Of course, neither the cat nor any other animal can see in total darkness, but cats have the ability to register light such that they can see under circumstances which seem pitch black to us.

After light has passed through the eye, any that has not been absorbed by the retinal cells strikes a reflecting layer at the back of the eye. This layer, called the *tapetum lucidum*, returns light through the retina, increasing the strength of the information recorded. This mirror-like layer makes the eyes of cats and other nocturnal animals appear to 'shine' in the dark, because it reflects back whatever light is available.

A cat may find bright lights dazzling, even when its iris is almost fully closed. This is because its eyes are designed to make the most of the dim light of night-time, dawn and dusk when it is hunting. To reduce the brightness, it may draw an extra eyelid, which is known as the *haw* or *nictitating membrane*, across the eye. This closes upwards from the inner corner of the eye, filtering the light. The membrane is not opaque and allows some vision. It protects the eye from damage and also helps to clean the eye. If it stays up for long periods, it is usually a sign of illness in a cat, but it does sometimes remain partially closed in cats which are enjoying perfectly good health.

The iris, the eye's dark centre, controls the amount of light which enters. In bright light, top, it narrows to a slit. In poor light, centre, it opens to a full circle. An extra eyelid, bottom, protects the eye from dazzling brightness.

Hearing

The cat can hear and interpret sounds over a range from 30 to 45,000 hertz, or cycles per second. This means that the cat can hear a far wider range of sounds than we can. Our optimum range is from about 2000 to 4000 hertz. Except for the very lowest notes, the hearing of cats and people is about equal up to 2000 hertz but then, even when our hearing is at its best, the cat's is even better. Few humans can hear notes above about 20,000 hertz, about the top note that can be played upon a violin. A cat's hearing, however, does not begin to fade until about 40,000 hertz and some cats seem able to register as high as 60,000. This means that cats can hear a whole world of sounds which are completely imperceptible to us.

A movement will catch a cat's eye only if it is within the field of vision, but a sound will attract its attention from anywhere within carrying distance. Practically no movement can occur without some sound being made. A cat can not only hear but also locate the movement, because its ears are shaped and ridged to concentrate the sound. The ears are also highly manoeuvrable so that they can focus on a particular sound source and place its location. For example, a lightly crumpled ball of paper falling behind a cat crackles as it lands. This provides the cat with a means of placing it exactly, although it has not seen it land. Cats distinguish and identify sounds with great precision. They identify the footsteps of a member of the family or a frequent visitor long before we hear them. They also readily recognize the sound of a particular car engine which is running outside the home.

The pitch of sound is measured in hertz (cycles per second). The adult human range of hearing is somewhat more than that of the octaves of a standard piano. Cats can hear sounds over a far wider range.

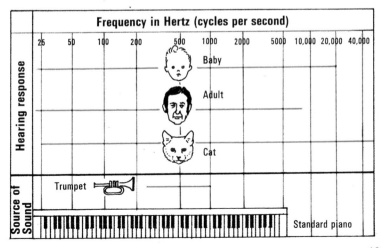

Balance

As well as transmitting sound signals to the brain, the structure of the inner ear also plays a part in balance. Cats do not seem to be affected by travel sickness from the movements of a ship or car, which many dogs and people experience and, because travel sickness is closely related to the sense of balance, it is possible that the formation of the inner ear is somewhat different in cats.

Landing on Four Feet

Cats can also right themselves as they fall through the air, so that they finally land squarely on four feet. This ability does not depend entirely upon sensations in the ear, because deaf cats can still right themselves. Even a cat without any inner ear has been known to do it. However, when this cat was blindfolded, it lost the ability to right itself. It is quite clear, therefore, that other senses are involved in this righting ability and sight is not the only one, because the pressure-sensitive cells which are scattered over the cat's body also seem to play a part.

It should not be thought that a cat can make a safe landing from every fall. For example, if it is dropped awkwardly from a child's arms, it might not have time and space to turn. It might right itself when falling from a great height, but the impact might cause serious damage to the limbs or to the jaw if it strikes the ground first. A cat asleep on a ledge or window-sill may also hurt itself if it turns and falls, because it may fail to wake up until it is too late to rotate in the air and land on its feet.

A sighted cat turns while falling and makes a four-footed landing.

14

Touch

We consciously touch things with our fingers and so we tend to associate the sense of touch with them. However, we also feel touch on every part of our bodies, although not with quite such sensitivity. The cat may use its front paws to investigate an object. They are particularly sensitive and quite a large area of the cat's brain is devoted to handling messages from them. The nose is also very sensitive to touch and areas particularly sensitive to pressure are situated all over the body. These areas will respond to even the slightest pressure.

People often say that a cat uses its whiskers to measure whether it can squeeze through a particular space, but this is not really the way in which the whiskers function. The whiskers, eyebrows and the long hairs on the back of the front paws are together known as the *vibrissae*. They are all sensitive to pressure, even minute variations in the pressure of the air around them which is affected by the presence of nearby objects. That is how the vibrissae are used for judging spaces. People also possess this awareness of pressure, but we rely much more on our other senses and are rarely very responsive to it, except perhaps when frightened and in the dark.

Smell

The cat's sense of smell is also highly developed. It does not seem to play an important role in tracking down prey, but it is a major means of identifying both things and living creatures. It is the sense used by the newborn kitten before its eyes are open to find its way to its mother's nipples. It is also an important way of communicating territorial and sexual

The cat has pressure-sensitive hairs, called vibrissae. These are the whiskers, the eyebrows and the long hairs on the backs of the front paws. The vibrissae aid the cat's spatial awareness, registering minute changes of pressure caused by the presence of objects and surfaces around it.

information. Every animal, and every person, has their individual odour. A cat will recognize friends or strangers by their smell. It will reject or even attack the unfamiliar which seems to threaten danger. A new kitten brought into a household will often be rejected as an outsider. However, it can be made acceptable if its smell is disguised. This can be done by rubbing it with something impregnated with the resident cat's smell, such as the bedding on which it usually sleeps. The most effective method is to use a little litter from the toilet tray which has absorbed the smell in the resident cat's urine.

A cat marks its claim to territory with its personal scent. It does this by spraying its urine against various places or by rubbing against them. In this way it deposits an identifying secretion from scent glands which are found by the anus, along the tail, around the lips and chin, and on either side of the forehead. Urine marking is largely the habit of adult males, although some females also do it. A male which has been neutered before reaching sexual maturity does not usually develop the habit. The urine is distinctive and easily recognizable, but most people do not notice the scent from the other glands, even though cats mark us when they rub against us. For example, our pet cat may also be marking us when it affectionately rubs its head against our hand, because it has scent glands on the side of its head. This marking does not leave an unpleasant smell. However, the scent contained in urine is extremely strong. Because it is unpleasant to most people, owners usually have male cats not required for breeding neutered to stop them spraying around the house. In fact it would be better if all tomcats not kept as studs were neutered. This also applies to females if their owners are not prepared to accept the trouble and expense of raising kittens and finding them homes. If this were general practice, thousands of unwanted kittens would not have to be destroyed each year.

When a female cat is ready to mate, she produces a different scent which conveys this information to any male in the neighbourhood. Although it is not so overpowering as the smell of a male's urine, it can be recognized by more sensitive human noses.

If you watch two cats meeting and greeting each other, you will usually find that they sniff at the areas on the other cat where the scent glands are situated. At the same time they rub against each other, leaving a scent marking. A cat will often sniff the clothing of a member of a household on his or her arrival home. Even luggage or shopping bags are of interest, because they will have picked up scents from the places where they have been. To the cat this sniffing must be rather like having a chat about the things that the person was doing while away from home.

Cats are sensual creatures. They enjoy warmth, whether lying by a fire, stretched on a boiler or basking in the sun. They like being stroked and gently scratched and tickled. They seem to enjoy smells for their own sake. They sometimes take great pleasure in sniffing at things which we might find objectionable and they will often sit by an open door or window, savouring the scents that waft past. To increase their scent awareness,

Smell is one of the most important of a cat's senses. Long before a kitten's eyes are open, smell guides it to its mother's nipples.

Smell is used to identify objects or their past presence. A cat will 'nose' out food and prey and investigate new objects, especially shopping which may contain its dinner.

Smell is used to mark territory and objects. When a cat rubs against a person's hand, glands on its head leave a scent behind.

they open their mouths and draw in air so that the smells not only activate the scent organs in the nose, but the air is also drawn up two ducts placed in the hard palate just behind the upper incisor teeth. These ducts lead to another olfactory organ. This feature is not exclusive to cats. Snakes and several other kinds of animals also possess it.

Language

Scent is one form of communication, but the cat also has a considerable vocal range. There are the chirrups and squeaks of kittens, the gentle noises and disciplinary calls of mother cats, the meow to attract attention and make demands on people, the special sounds made during courtship and the caterwauling of the male and the calling of the female in season. There are spits and growls, hisses and screams. There is the purr of contentment, a short, purr-like noise which usually seems to be a comment and a deep purr which can sometimes indicate pain. All cats seem to understand generalized warning and sexual signals and mothers and kittens sometimes seem to convey definite messages in sound, far beyond reminders of mealtimes or cries of 'I'm lost, please find me'. Many owners believe that they can interpret a large part of their cat's vocabulary and cats certainly seem able to link human speech with certain meanings, so that the owner and pet appear to converse with one another. However, little is known, scientifically, about feline vocal communication beyond more obvious generalizations.

Body Language

Scent and vocal signals are not the only means of communication. Most animals, and people too, also use what is often called 'body language'. For example, postures, often unconsciously, indicate attitudes. In cats this is particularly noticeable when two cats confront each other. By making its fur stand on end and positioning itself to look as large and formidable as possible, a cat makes a show of strength towards another cat. The other cat, if it is prepared to give way without a contest, makes itself as small as

Cats are patient hunters and will wait in ambush or carefully stalk their prey, making themselves as inconspicuous as possible.

By making its fur stand on end, a cat seeks to appear more formidable.
When it rolls on its back, its belly is vulnerable but, in this position, it
can lash out with its powerful back legs.

possible, crouching low, dropping its head and being entirely submissive. Often an exchange of threatening displays, with plenty of hissing and growling, will end with one cat giving way. However, should both cats hold their ground, they may lash out at each other with their claws, at first only symbolically while keeping out of range, and then in earnest. A cat which is doing badly may roll over on its back, exposing its unprotected belly and becoming apparently submissive. However, if the other cat pursues the attack, it will lash out with its powerful back feet which it cannot use when standing up. In this way it can deliver severe blows to the aggressor above.

The tail is an easily interpreted indicator of a cat's mood. When the cat is relaxed and happy, the tail is carried high in the air with the tip just slightly curled, like a banner of welcome as it comes to greet you. When agitated or annoyed, the cat will swish its tail from side to side. A twitching tail tip usually indicates concentration and interest. Erect ears indicate similar emotions.

The Hunter

The cat's keen senses and efficient body are designed to serve it in finding and obtaining food. The cat eats meat and, because it is a hunter rather than a scavenger, its eyes and ears are tuned to locating prey, while its

Cats usually kill their prey by severing the spinal cord at the back of the neck with their teeth. If kittens are not exposed to live prey, they may never learn this killing bite.

limbs, sharp teeth and powerful claws are adapted to catching and killing it.

The cat is patient. It will wait for hours along a route where it knows that suitable prey will pass, waiting for the precise moment to pounce and kill. It stalks with stealth, keeping to cover or running almost flattened to the ground in exposed places. It will freeze, quite motionless, to avoid betraying its position. Caution and care increase as it approaches its prey. Ears and tail are kept low so that they will not betray its position, but few cats can suppress an excited twitch of the tail tip. After a trembling quiver passes through the hindquarters, there is a final dash and the victim will be struck down. Sometimes the cat lands close to its victim, keeping its hind feet on the ground to give stability against resistance and lunging forward to grip its prey on the back of the neck with a fatal bite. That is the way in which a cat usually catches rodents and other small animals which often form its prey, although sometimes it leaps down on them from above.

To catch birds, the cat must suppress its instinct to pause and pounce, which is something that not all cats can do, because birds can fly away between the cat's dash forwards and the final spring. Cats will leap to snatch a bird in its jaws as it flies away or strike it with a paw to knock it to the ground. Although cats have a reputation for catching birds, only a few are skilled at it. Cats catch insects in their jaws or swat them down and eat them while they are still stunned. Some cats even learn to fish. They dip a paw into the water and flip a fish on to the bank where they can

Some cats can fish. They dip a paw into the water and, when a fish swims above it, they flip it upwards, out of the water and on to the bank where it can be gripped with the claws.

grasp it firmly.

A cat administers its killing bite with its four large canine teeth. These teeth are also useful for tearing flesh. Between them are sharp little incisors and, farther back, the molars, which are used for cutting food between their scissor-like, serrated surfaces. A cat often holds its head sideways to its food, using the molars to cut off a piece of meat. None of the teeth are really used for grinding, in the way that human teeth are. The rough surface of the cat's tongue is also used, like a rasp, to strip meat from bones.

The cat's other sharp weapons, its claws, are continually growing. Those on the front paws are highly efficient. A single claw can be used to hook on to something. A sheath covers the outer part of each front claw. This is shed when it loses its sharp point to reveal another sharp point beneath. The claws on the rear feet are not as sharp. To keep them in trim, the cat chews at the blunted and frayed edges caused by wear. When a cat scratches against the trunk of a tree, or a piece of furniture, it is not actually sharpening its claws as many people think. Instead it is removing the outer sheaths and generally exercising the mechanism by which the claws are extended and retracted into the paw and stretching and exercising its legs. If you do not want your cat to damage your furniture, you should choose a scratching place and train the cat to use it from kittenhood. It might be an old chair, a log or a scratching post covered in a coarse and tough fabric, such as hessian, which is not found elsewhere in the house.

Training and Learning

Much of the cat's hunting behaviour is instinctive, but it seems that the method of killing prey by biting it in the neck has to be taught. Mother cats sometimes bring back live prey to their kittens as a means of teaching them. All the techniques of hunting and fighting can be seen in the play of kittens as they ambush, chase and fight each other. However, some built-in behaviour pattern prevents them taking their games too far so that no serious injury will be inflicted. Often a game will suddenly stop and kittens will change roles. A kitten pretending to be the prey changes places and becomes the hunter. The games which adult pet cats play are also closely related to hunting. Chasing, pouncing, catching and re-trieving may be applied to a ball, a piece of string or a crumpled piece of paper, but these activities employ the same skills as those used by the wild cat in catching its prey and defending itself.

Except for Siamese, which are frequently precocious, kittens do not open their eyes till they are about nine days old and they cannot stand or walk well enough to wander far from the nest until they are about three weeks old. About a week later, they start to eat some solid food and the weaning process begins.

When the kittens are small, their mother will massage their anuses and genital areas to encourage them to excrete and wash them clean. When they begin to leave the nest, they will probably copy their mother in using a litter tray. However, it may be a little longer before they will copy her if she performs her toilet out of doors. They will also learn to wash them-selves and each other. The cat uses its tongue and paws as a sort of scrubbing brush and face cloth. Its tongue can reach most of its coat

In playing together, kittens develop and practise the skills which they will need to catch prey and to defend themselves.

A cat's tongue can reach all parts except its head and neck.

directly, but it cleans its face and the top of its head by wetting its paws with its tongue and rubbing vigorously with them.

Kittens should not leave their mother for a new home until they are at least eight weeks old. By then they should be pretty independent, fully weaned and house-trained. On arrival, if you show them their litter tray, they will generally use it from the start and, after the excitement of the journey, they may need to use it right away. To begin with, give them the same diet as they had where they were born, then make changes gradually. At first they will probably have four meals a day, because kittens have tiny stomachs and cannot eat much at one time. In a month or so, you can cut down to three meals a day and, when the kittens are six months old, you can give them two meals a day. Later on some owners give them only one large meal. Kittens should eat as much as they want while they are growing, but an adult cat usually needs about one small can of cat food, or its equivalent, every day. Fresh water should also always be available for kittens and adult cats.

A new kitten may feel lonely without its mother, brothers and sisters. Once the excitement of being somewhere new gives way to the realization that it is on its own, the kitten will require a lot of comfort and reassurance. Talk to it quietly and make it feel welcome in your home, ensuring that other pets do not become jealous of or aggressive towards it. However, a kitten must not be spoiled. Start calling it by name and use a name which is easily said and easily recognizable. Decide on the rules you expect it to live by and be a gentle disciplinarian from the start. It is no use expecting a cat to understand that a misdemeanour you found amusing one day is forbidden the next.

THE STORY OF THE CAT

When was the cat first domesticated? No one knows the answer to this question. Or, rather, it might be more accurate to say that the cat has never been properly domesticated. It still retains an independent spirit and seems to share our lives on its own terms.

Another domestic animal, the dog, is a pack animal. It threw in its lot with man and joined his nomadic hunting bands far back in prehistoric times. The cat, however, hunts alone. It was not until man became a farmer and began to lead a settled life in the Neolithic period that human society can have offered it any advantage.

Although this is only a theory, and there is no firm evidence to support it, the turning point may have come when farmers gathered their harvests and stored their grain. Grain stores would have attracted large numbers of mice and rats and it was perhaps these animals which caught the attention of cats.

And then, perhaps, the Neolithic people realized that cats did them no harm, but they did keep down the pests which ate their grain. In fact the earliest evidence firmly linking cats with man comes from Ancient Egypt, which gained its wealth and power from the grain grown in the fertile Nile valley.

Left: The Egyptian goddess Bast has a cat's head and kittens at her feet. She holds a rattle-like sistrum, a rhythm instrument used by her worshippers and an aegis, a small ceremonial basket.

In a 3,200-year-old papyrus of the Book of the Dead, the Sun god Ra, in cat form, is shown slaying Apep, the serpent of darkness. The ancient Egyptians believed that this ritual was repeated every dawn.

Cats in Ancient Egypt

An Egyptian tomb contains a picture of a cat painted in about 2600 BC. It is wearing a wide collar, but it may be a captured wild cat and not a domesticated animal. The first unchallenged evidence of domesticated cats, however, does not appear until about 800 years later, although the cat was an important animal in Ancient Egypt long before that. It was associated with a number of Egyptian gods and a cult developed around it.

The Egyptians did not worship the cat as such, but they imagined some of their gods in cat form. The Sun god Ra took the form of a cat to overcome darkness in the form of the serpent Apep. A drawing on a papyrus shows the Ra-cat wielding a knife to gain the victory which is repeated at dawn every day, because Ra and Apep are immortal. Another snake-killing deity, the goddess Mafdet, was also depicted in cat form in pyramid carvings. These show her as the protectress of the pharaoh. Cats do attack snakes—you have only to see their reaction to a moving piece of string or a sash being wriggled across the floor to see that instinct revived. Hence these religious symbols may have reflected a role that some cats played in life, protecting Egyptians from serpents in the home. Again we have no firm evidence for this theory. It should also be remembered that snakes also held an important role in Egyptian religion, as did various other animals, including hawks, hippopotamuses, ibises, jackals, lions and monkeys. Each Egyptian god and goddess had a cult animal which was kept in the sanctuary of their temple as their representation in physical form. They were also carved and moulded in animal shape, or with animal heads, as religious figures and protective amulets.

Bast and Sekhmet, two goddesses who were linked with the Sun god Ra, were worshipped in the temple of the Sun at Heliopolis, the main centre of Sun worship in Ancient Egypt. At first the goddesses were shown with lions' heads, but Bast was presented later as a cat or with a cat's head. Sekhmet, the Big Cat, was seen as the searing, destroying power of the Sun. Bast (or Pasht or Bastet as she is sometimes called), the Little Cat, was a kindly force, representing the Sun's life-giving aspect.

At Bubastis, which became Bast's great cult centre on the Lower Nile, evidence of her worship goes back to earlier than 1780 BC. She still had devotees when the Roman Emperor Theodosius suppressed paganism in AD 392. This represents a span of at least 2100 years, which is longer than Christianity has existed. The temple cats at Bubastis lived in a court-yard tended by officials, who passed down the honour from father to son. The priests watched the cats for any sign that indicated a message from the goddess. A worshipper seeking the support or intervention of the goddess shaved the head of his child and took the shorn locks to the temple where they were weighed. He then presented a balancing weight of silver to the guardian of the cats, who fed them an offering of fish.

Both temple and domestic cats were given the funeral rites of Ancient Egypt. Many people had their cats buried at Bubastis where extensive catacombs were found lined with hundreds of thousands of dead cats, embalmed and mummified and ranged on tiered shelves. No value was placed on these finds when they were excavated and they were used as fertilizer. As a result only a few survived. In 1952 a crate of mummies was discovered in the British Museum. This crate had been brought from Giza (not Bubastis) some 50 years earlier. It contained 192 mummified cats, 7 mongooses, 3 dogs and a fox. Four of the cats were indentified as Jungle Cats (*Felis chaus*), while the rest seemed to be a halfway stage between the African Wild Cat (*Felis libyca*) and the modern domestic cat.

It was not only temple cats that were held in high regard. To harm any cat might result in severe punishment and, if a pet cat died, all the house-hold shaved off their eyebrows in mourning. One painting shows a cat pouncing upon wildfowl among the papyrus reeds of the Nile delta. On a boat a man stands with a boomerang-stick in his hand, about to throw it. This seems sufficient evidence that the Egyptians trained cats as retrievers. According to the Greek writer Plutarch (AD 46-120), the Egyptians of his time took great care to ensure that female cats were mated with males of a compatible character. The Egyptians guarded their cats jealously. Laws forbade their export, although some found their way abroad, smuggled perhaps by Phoenician traders.

Opposite: An Egyptian wall painting from a tomb in Thebes shows a man hunting for wildfowl from a papyrus boat. He is using a boomerang to strike down the birds which his cat is retrieving.

Cats in Greece and Rome

The Greeks do not seem to have been very enthusiastic about cats. There are almost no surviving references in literature, although one poet from Rhodes makes a character remark to an Egyptian: 'If you see a sick cat you weep for it. As far as I'm concerned, I'll happily kill it for its skin.' There is a Greek carving on a statue base which shows men with a cat and a dog, both on leads, which they seem to be encouraging to fight. However, at least one Athenian cat seems to have been loved, because it appears on the funeral stone of its master.

Cats also appear in one or two vase paintings from the Greek colonies in Italy. It was the Romans, however, who adopted the cat enthusiastically as a pet and, along with other Egyptian religions and fashions, as a religious symbol too. The Romans recognized the value of cats in protecting gardens from mice and moles and keeping rats away from food stores. They probably introduced the cat to the far provinces of the empire, including Britain.

Egypt and Rome were not the only societies with religions that revered the cat. In China one of the gods of agriculture took cat form. In South America the Peruvians had a cat-like god of copulation. Other members of the cat family featured in Aztec and Inca religions. In Ireland there was a cat-headed god and one Scandinavian goddess had a chariot drawn by cats. The sacrifice of a cat and even the eating of a cat featured in fertility rites to ensure a good harvest in some parts of Europe.

This carving is on a statue base, dating from before 480 BC. It was found embedded in the ancient city wall of Athens. It shows a group of young Greeks apparently enticing a cat and a dog to fight. However, some people dispute that the animal on the right is a cat.

Cats and Witchcraft

The Romans tended to identify the Egyptian goddess Bast with Artemis or Diana, goddess of the Moon. She, in turn, became identified with Hecate, chief of the witches. The cat seemed to the Christian Church to be linked with paganism and churchmen sought to suppress the power its image exercised. As late as the end of the 15th century, Pope Innocent VII issued instructions for the Inquisition to seek out cat worshippers. Medieval French peasants believed that cats slept during the day so that at night they might perform their duty of warning evil spirits of any intruder, giving them time to disappear. Many thought that the Devil himself would appear as a cat, often as a black one. Some members of the religious and military order of the Knights Templars, who served in the crusades, admitted under torture that they had worshipped the Devil in this form.

The appearance of the Devil as a black cat was said to have caused an outbreak of the nervous disease St Vitus' Dance in Metz, France, in 1344. On June 24, for more than 400 years thereafter, 13 cats were burned alive in the town square. A similar ceremony took place in Luxembourg. In Paris on the next day, the Feast of St John, a barrel or sack of live cats was burned in the Place de Grève. A bonfire and the date, Midsummer Day, suggest a pre-Christian connection. However, the symbolism of these and other ceremonies, like those in the Belgian town of Ypres, where cats were flung from a belfry, and at Store Magleby, near Copenhagen,

This 17th-century woodcut shows three witches, Anne Baker, Joan Willimot and Ellen Green, from Leicestershire in central England. In her confession in 1618 Ellen claimed that Joan had given her two spirits, a cat and a mole. A dog, an owl and a rat are also shown here as familiars.

where horsemen tilted at a barrel containing a live cat, was that people were ridding themselves of evil, personified by the cats. The Christian Church's persecution of the cat, however, enabled the rat population in Europe to increase. It was, in part, responsible for the spread of rat-carried plagues.

Cruelty to cats also occurred in Britain. At the coronation of Elizabeth I, an effigy of the Pope was carried in procession. Inside it were caged live cats. When the effigy was burned upon a pyre, the screams of the poor animals were said to represent the cries of devils within the body of the Pope.

While people in continental Europe generally believed that the Devil might appear as a cat or that a witch might transform herself into a cat, many in Britain thought that cats and other small animals were the form in which a Devil servant might attend a witch. They believed that all witches had such a 'familiar', and many a pet kept by some lonely old lady led to accusations of witchcraft. Such accusations reached their peak towards the end of the reign of Elizabeth I and during that of James I of England (James VI of Scotland), who made himself something of an authority on witchcraft. Witch mania spread to the English colonies in North America and was responsible for witchcraft trials, including the famous ones at Salem, Massachusetts, in 1692.

Cats as Companions
The Church's attitude towards cats was not paramount even in Europe.

If it had been, there would have been no need for persecution. The idea that cats could bring good luck survived in folk cultures. In southern France, particularly, people believed in magician cats, known as *matagots*, which brought good fortune and prosperity to a house where they were received lovingly and hospitably. Such cats appear in folklore from many parts of the world. Most famous are probably Puss in Boots, who earned his master a kingdom, and Dick Whittington's cat, who made his master a rich merchant and Lord Mayor of London. Whittington was a real Lord Mayor, but the story seems to be an anglicized version of what was originally a Persian tale.

Not all churchmen were against the cat. It was the only companion allowed to anchoresses (female recluses) under the discipline of the Cistercian order. The 6th-century Pope Gregory I's only companion when he retired to monastic life was a cat. An Irish monk, whose life's work was copying manuscripts, wrote a poem in Irish about his cat:

'I and Pangur Ban, my cat
'Tis a like task we are at;
Hunting mice is his delight,
Hunting words I sit all night . . .'

Welsh law of the 10th century set high value on cats and, 100 years earlier, Henry I of Saxony had decreed that anyone who killed an adult cat should be fined 60 bushels of corn. The usefulness of the cat as a rodent-catcher was never completely overlooked. Those who most valued the cat's help, those free from superstition or those too powerful to fear the accusation of witchcraft sometimes grew attached to their pets. Another Pope, Leo XII, had a cat called Micetto, which was born in the Loggia of Raphael in the Vatican. It was brought up in the fold of his robes and it sat with him when he gave audiences. Cardinal Wolsey had a cat which accompanied him to services. At one time Cardinal Richelieu had at least 14 cats, with which he used to play each morning.

Prelates, monarchs and statesmen are all numbered among cat lovers. President Theodore Roosevelt had a cat called Slippers which went to White House dinners. Winston Churchill had a ginger tom which sometimes attended meetings of the British Cabinet in World War II. Another British prime minister Harold Wilson took the family Siamese with him to Downing Street. The French prime minister Georges Clemenceau kept a Blue Persian at the Elysée Palace. The Italian dictator Benito Mussolini and the Russian revolutionary leader Vladimir Lenin are also numbered among cat-loving politicians.

As any cat owner knows, their affection and loyalty are returned by their pets. When William Shakespeare's patron, Henry Wriothesley, 3rd Earl of Southampton, was sent to the Tower of London after his involvement in a rising against Elizabeth I, his pet cat found a way to join him. It made its way into the Tower and climbed down a chimney to get into the room where the Earl was confined. An earlier prisoner in the

Tower, Sir Henry Wyat, was befriended by a cat which caught pigeons for him to supplement his meagre rations. Another prisoner was the 18th-century poet Christopher Smart, who was confined to a madhouse. There he found a companion in a cat called Jeoffrey, who inspired part of a famous poem.

Many literary figures from classical times to the present have loved cats and written about them. Dr Samuel Johnson bought oysters for his cat Hodge. The French writer Colette often wrote with a cat at her elbow. Charles Dickens, William Makepeace Thackeray, Honoré de Balzac . . . . . the list could go on for ever. There are also many poems and stories about cats ranging from Aesop's *Fables* to Lewis Carroll's Cheshire Cat and from Edward Lear's Foss to Don Marquis's alley cat Mehitabel.

Painters and sculptors, from the ancient Egyptians to such great masters as Pieter Brueghel and Leonardo da Vinci, and the cartoonists Ronald Searle and Kliban have portrayed cats. Some artists, such as Theophile Steinlen and Louis Wain, have specialized in drawing cats. Many of Louis Wain's paintings of cats were reproduced as postcards and these cards are now prized by many collectors.

Cats in the East

One artist who obviously loved cats and liked to include them in his paintings and woodblock prints was the Japanese master Kuniyoshi (1797-1861). He painted cats in domestic settings and cats behaving like humans in everyday life. At least five of his self-portraits include one of the several cats which lived in his studio. He also used cats to illustrate proverbs and portrayed cats from the myths and legends of Japan.

The Japanese, like the Europeans, believed that witches could be cats, but they thought that the cat turned itself into a human rather than the opposite transformation. They also believed in Devil cats which could be recognized easily because they had forked tails. However, cats could bring good luck too, especially tortoiseshell cats. Sailors especially liked to have a tortoiseshell aboard. They believed that it could warn of approaching storms and that it could frighten storm demons away if it was sent up to the top of the ship's mast.

According to legend the first cat in Japan was introduced by the 10th-century Emperor Ichijo, although cats were probably known there several hundred years earlier. It was a white cat from China and, when it gave birth to five pure white kittens in the imperial palace at Kyoto, the emperor ordered that they should be brought up with as much care as children of the imperial family.

Cats became pampered pets in Japan. Statues and pottery figures of cats were given the task of protecting crops and silkworms from mice and rats. Understandably they did not do the job well. Eventually a law was passed at the beginning of the 17th century, which ordered that all adult cats should be set free. It also forbade the selling of cats or even giving them as presents. Cats were again given the chance to demonstrate their hunting skills and earn a place in every kind of home. Perhaps because the

One of Sir John Tenniel's illustrations for Lewis Carroll's children's classic Alice's Adventures in Wonderland (1865) *shows Alice with the Cheshire Cat which slowly vanishes, its grin disappearing last of all. Carroll described some characteristic cat behaviour as follows:*

' "Well, then" the Cat went on, "you see a dog growls when it's angry, and wags its tail when it's pleased. Now I growl when I'm pleased, and wag my tail when I'm angry. Therefore I'm mad."

"I call it purring, not growling," said Alice. "Call it what you like," said the Cat.'

Japanese empire rejected contact with the outside world and became isolated, a breed of cat, the Japanese Bobtail, which is quite different from any other cat in the world, developed in Japan. The Japanese do not consider it to be special and it appears in pictures and prints dating back many years. Its special difference is the shortness of its tail (see pages 120-121).

While cats aroused the antagonism of many in the Christian Church, cats seem to have been welcome in eastern religions. The Birman breed is said to have its origins in the temple cats of south-eastern Asia (see page 90) and every temple in Japan had its cats to protect sacred manuscripts from attack by rodents. The guardian cat of one lowly temple is said to have attracted the attention of travellers on a nearby high road. She lured them to visit her temple so that they would make an offering at it. The cat soon became famous and her temple wealthy. Today this temple in Tokyo has beside it a cat cemetery which is renowned among

In southern France, people once believed in magician cats, called matagots. *Puss in Boots, shown here in an engraving by the French artist Gustave Doré (1832-83), is one of the best known stories of a* matagot *who, by his cunning, brought his poor master fame and fortune. The story appears in the folk culture of many nations, although the* matagot *is not always a cat.*

Japanese cat lovers, who bring offerings to the temple to ensure their own pet's entry into heaven. The facade of the temple is lined with pictures of its famous servant shown with one paw raised in a welcoming gesture. This picture has become a symbol of good luck.

A Unique Pet

Demons or guardians, rodent-catchers or pampered pets, cats can still arouse controversy. Some people cannot stand them, sometimes with good reason because some are unfortunate enough to be allergic to a cat's soft fur. However, even those who claim that they do not like cats have to admit to their intelligence and beauty. For those who love cats, they are much more than merely elegant and clever. They can be wicked and deceitful, sometimes savage and spiteful, but they are endlessly resourceful, comforting and understanding. They offer companionship, amusement and a cuddly sensuality which no other animal can match. To those who have lived with an affectionate cat, life will never again seem quite complete without the warmth of the cat's furry body and the murmur of its contented purring. As the American Mark Twain said: 'A home without a cat, and a well-fed, well-petted and properly revered cat, may be a perfect home, *perhaps*, but how can it prove its title?'

THE DEVELOPMENT OF BREEDS

All modern varieties of the domestic cat belong to the same species. They are closely related to the wild cats of the Old World, but zoologists argue over exactly how to categorize those relationships. The issue is complicated by the fact that domestic cats can interbreed with wild cats. Some taxonomists put both the European Wild Cat (*Felis silvestris*) and the African Wild Cat (*Felis libyca*) into the same species, making the two kinds subspecies together with the domestic cat. The European Wild Cat is not limited to Europe, but ranges across Asia as far as China. The African Wild Cat, also known as the Kaffir Cat, is found as far east as South-East Asia, including India. Some experts consider that the European Wild Cat should be ruled out as a possible ancestor of the domestic cat because of differences in their skulls. The evidence of Egyptian mummies also gives support to the view that the African Wild Cat is the ancestor of the domestic cat (see page 26), although mummies of the Jungle Cat (*Felis chaus*), which ranges from Egypt across to Vietnam, suggests that it was also domesticated. The Chinese Desert Cat (*Felis bieti*) of the Far East and other regional species may also have interbred with domestic animals and so they, too, may have contributed to the development of the domestic cat in certain areas.

Early Domestic Cats
The first known domestic cats appeared in Egypt. They were probably taken from Africa to Europe and, thence, around the world, although it

Both the European Wild Cat and the African Wild Cat can interbreed with the domestic cat, which probably developed from the African Wild Cat.

European
Wild Cat

African
Wild Cat

has been suggested that cats were already domesticated in China by 1000 BC. This implies that they may have been domesticated independently in the East. No evidence exists to explain why the basic short-haired type became the common cat of Europe, while a long-haired form appeared in the Middle East and a rather more svelte body shape developed in the Far East.

Paintings, carvings and mosaics from ancient times tell us what some individual cats looked like. Egyptian cats are depicted with stripes and spots like those of the African Wild Cat and the Jungle Cat, which both have very variable coats today. Sometimes they look quite plump, but they usually have rather long legs, long, slim tails and big ears. The few Greek images of cats also look rather sinuous. Mosaics from Rome and Pompeii, which was destroyed in AD 79, show striped cats—the tabby

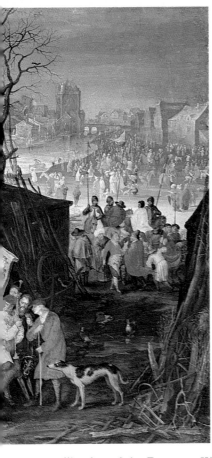

'The Adoration of the Kings', which was painted in 1598 by Jan Brueghel I (1568-1625) shows a cat looking down from a vantage point above the stable. The blue-grey coat of this cat is perhaps typical of the type of cats common in Europe during the Middle Ages.

pattern, like that of the European Wild Cat, which is passed on more readily than other coat patterns.

Medieval carvings and manuscript illuminations sometimes show animals which we recognize as cats more by the fact that they are catching mice than by the accuracy of their portrayal. However, by the 16th century, painters were producing realistic pictures of cats showing them in all kinds of domestic situations. Leonardo da Vinci included a cat in studies of the Virgin and Child and cats often appear in domestic scenes painted by artists of the Dutch and Flemish schools. These cats often turn out to be tabbies. However, it is intriguing to discover that, despite the dominance of the tabby pattern, the English antiquarian John Aubrey referred to two tabby cats presented to Archbishop Laud in the 1630s as though they were valuable rarities. He described the 'common English

Cat (as) . . . white with some blewish piedness: sc. a gallipot blew. The race or breed of them are now almost lost'. Aubrey wrote this at a later date when tabbies, or 'Cyprus-catts', as he said they were first called, had become quite common. Another English writer, Edward Topsell, wrote a book about animals which was published in 1607. In it he said 'Cats are of divers colours, but for the most part griseld, like to congealed ice', although he singled out black cats as coming from Spain and reproduced a woodcut of a striped tabby.

Descriptions like 'congealed ice' and 'gallipot blew' suggest the shade of grey coat colour that cat fanciers call blue. It is reported that the proportion of blue cats in London has declined rapidly over the last 150 years, while the proportion in the North American cat population seems to be much higher than in Britain. Various suggestions have been made to explain such local differences. It has been claimed that, once established, a cat population breeding freely without human interference maintains the same balance of colours and patterns, although there is a greater tendency to change in cities, where darker coloured coats are more frequently seen. Because of the greater and earlier urbanization in Europe, experts have suggested that the balance in the modern American cat population could approximate to that of the mid-17th century in Europe, when the American cats were first taken across the Atlantic Ocean from the Old World.

Around the beginning of the 18th century, the French naturalist Georges Buffon suggested that certain parts of the world produced cats of certain colours. For example, South Africa was credited with blue cats, like the breed the French already knew as the Chartreux. Indeed some say that the Chartreux was imported from southern Africa. Spanish cats

The Egyptians revered the cat goddess, but artists also portrayed cats with humour. In this papyrus from Cairo Museum, cats act as nursemaids to baby mice and as hairdresser to Lady Mouse.

were often described as red, black and white, their colours strengthening to black rather than brown, and white rather than grey, whereas it was thought that colours became lighter in Syria. Another suggestion was that hot climates helped to create permanent varieties. Buffon also referred to a Chinese cat with long hair and pendulous ears, although in a supplement added some years later he commented that this might be another species which he called a Sumxu, which was a domesticated animal and very like a cat.

It would be a mistake to treat all these old ideas as scientifically sound. However, long-haired cats, which first appeared in Europe in the 16th century, do seem to have been introduced from the Middle East. Buffon referred to the Chorozan from Persia, which he described as a blue-grey long-hair, and the Angora, which he suggested came from Syria. Certain types of cat reached Europe and North America from particular places and they are discussed later in this book. However, the movement of cats around the world with man and the possible interbreeding with wild cats have now produced a wide range of type and colour possibilities for the domestic cat and these are quite unrelated to geography.

The First Cat Shows

Although the new and exotic attracted attention in the 17th and 18th centuries, it was not until the 19th century that a large number of people began to take an interest in the breeding of particular types of cat to conform to any agreed standards of excellence and to judge them against each other.

The first real cat show to be held anywhere in the world took place at the Crystal Palace in London in 1871, and 170 cats were exhibited in competition. To organize an event on that scale, some kind of loose affiliation must have existed between cat owners and fanciers. However, it was not until 1887 that the first major cat club was established. This was the National Cat Club, which began a stud book and register of cats. The first cat show in the United States took place in 1884. It formed part of a larger pet and livestock show. Another show in New York in 1895, which was organized by an Englishman, was the first devoted solely to cats. The first American cat club, the Beresford Cat Club of Chicago, was established in 1889.

Cat Associations

In the 20th century the Cat Fancy, as the general body of people interested in cats and cat breeding is known, has grown throughout the world. Many clubs and organizations have been established to arrange shows and to advance the interests of their members. In Britain these are all gathered under one national organization, the Governing Council of the Cat Fancy, which was set up in 1910. In North America, however, a number of rival cat associations have grown up in Canada and the United States. In Europe, too, there are numerous independent associations. Fifteen or so are linked in the *Fédération Internationale Féline de l'Europe*,

The first real cat show was held in London in 1871.

ranging across a dozen countries, but others remain quite independent. The rest of the world has its own organizations, some of which are linked to the British body.

Each of these organizations decides what types of cat it recognizes as officially acceptable and lays down detailed descriptions for each breed which their members try to match in their cats.

Cat breeders register their cats and their cats' offspring with the organization to which they belong. They are issued with certificates in return. In this way a record is made of the extended ancestry of all cats under the control of that organization. Such information will also be recorded on a form which shows, at least, the later stages of the cat's pedigree, or family tree.

All cats have a pedigree—if anyone has bothered to keep a record of it. Usually, however, the term pedigree is used only of those cats that are pure-bred, with ancestors of several generations of the same breed and conforming to the description, or standard, laid down by the cat organizations. In general the standards of one association are very close to those of others, but they may differ in small details. Some associations also recognize a type as an official breed which other organizations do not. There are a number of broad groups recognized in North America which are not recognized in Britain and some European cats are not known in North America.

Changing Standards
The standards for some of the earliest breeds have changed somewhat over the years. New breeds and colour varieties have been introduced. This

has sometimes been done by bringing in cats from abroad, sometimes by developing a type which appeared quite accidentally as a quirk of nature, and sometimes by deliberately trying to create a new type by controlled cross-breeding. Each organization has its own rules about accepting a new colour or type of cat as an official breed. Recognition depends ·on such factors as the number of generations over which the type can be shown to have bred true and the number of cats of the type registered with the association. Details of all currently recognized varieties are given on pages 46-121 of this book.

Genetics and Breeding

The structure and shape of every living thing is determined by instructions contained in the living cell inherited from both parents at the moment of conception or fertilization. This information is carried in every cell of a cat's body by structures, called *chromosomes*, within the nucleus of the cell. Each cell has 19 pairs of chromosomes and each chromosome carries a set of *genes*, each of which corresponds with its opposite number on its paired chromosome. The genes are the instructions which the new life follows.

Within the body, as each cell divides to reproduce itself in the process of physical growth and replacement, the chromosomes and their genetic information are duplicated. In the reproductive cells, which unite at mating to produce the next generation, only half of the genes are duplicated, one from each pair. As a result, when these reproductive cells unite to produce the new kitten, they together produce a new set of 38, 19 from each parent. The kitten will develop according to the instructions contained in those 38 cells together.

The genetic coding of male and female animals differs in that the female has all 19 pairs of chromosomes made up of identical pairs, while the male has 18 identical pairs and one pair that does not match, which are known as the X and Y chromosomes. Females have two X chromosomes. When the male cell divides in sperm production, one-half will carry the X and one-half the Y chromosome. The sex of a kitten will depend on whether the fertilizing male sperm carries an X or Y chromosome. If it carries an X chromosome, it will unite with a female X to make XX and produce a female. If it is Y, it unites to form XY and produce a male.

Some genetic information is carried only on the X chromosomes. The instructions for red coat colour in cats is an example. This links inheritance of certain characteristics to a particular sex.

Sometimes the effects of radiation from an atomic explosion, a nuclear reactor or even an X-ray machine can change or damage a genetic tissue, causing a variation, or *mutation*, in the instructions it carries. This process can also happen spontaneously. It then becomes the mechanism by which natural evolution occurs. Except for these occasions, a kitten will always reflect the characteristics of its parents. However, those characteristics may not always be apparent, because genes do not all exert the same strength of control.

Dominant and Recessive Genes

Some genes are said to be dominant, while others are recessive. Dominant genes will tend to override any contradictory instruction coming from the matching gene from the other parent. Recessive genes will tend to give way, although the information will still be carried in every cell. As a result, if it meets a pairing gene in a later generation, its instructions will be followed. There are also instances where information of equal strength can result in midway instruction.

In cats short hair tends to be dominant over long hair. Hairlessness and rex-type coats (pages 69-70) are recessive. The colour white is dominant over all other colours. Why then are there not more white cats about? Perhaps it is because white makes a cat more noticeable and so it is less successful as a hunter. Perhaps it is also connected with the fact that a combination of a completely white coat and blue eyes often also carries a genetic patterning for deafness. Most non-pedigree white cats probably carry paired genes for some other colour and pure white pedigree cats are likely to be mated only to each other. You will, however, see many cats with large areas of white on the coat or with white spots. White is extremely difficult to eliminate once it has been introduced into a breeding line. It persists particularly around the chin or the throat and chest and, although it is not so dominant, on the paws and to a lesser extent on the lower part of the body. Of the other coat colours, black is dominant over all except white and red.

An all-over (solid or self-colour) coat is dominant over the Siamese-type restriction of colour to distinct parts of the body. Tabby patterning is dominant over non-tabby. Some genes also dilute the strength of the other colours, making black become chocolate or blue and red become cream.

The blue coat of the kitten, left, is a dilute form of black coat colour. White cats with blue eyes usually carry a linked tendency to deafness. However, if the kitten has a touch of colour in its coat, like the grey patch between this kitten's ears, its hearing may be sound. When the cat becomes an adult, the patch will disappear and it will look like an all-white cat.

Dominant	Recessive	Result
Short-hair	Long-hair	Short-hair
White	Black	White
White	Siamese	White
Black	Blue	Black
Tabby	Black	Tabby

When a dominant and a recessive gene are paired, as in the diagram, the offspring will have the coat or pattern of the dominant gene. The other information is carried in recessive form to be passed on to later generations.

Effects of Genetics

A great deal of research has been and is still being carried out into cat genetics and detailed information can be obtained from specialist publications. Some idea of the way in which it operates may be obtained from some examples.

For instance, a black cat from a line of black cats mated to a tabby from a line of tabbies will produce all tabby kittens. However, if those offspring, which all carry genes for both black and tabby, are then mated with each other, they will produce three tabbies for every one black kitten. If those kittens are then mated to pure black cats, the ratio of black to tabby will probably be one to one.

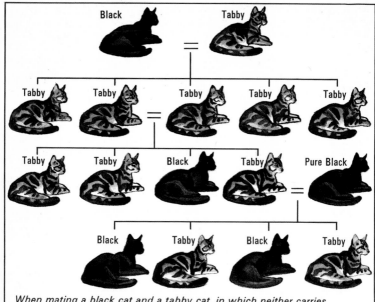

When mating a black cat and a tabby cat, in which neither carries recessive genes for colour, all the kittens will be tabbies, but this generation will carry both genes and the black may reappear in the next generation. If one of this third generation is then mated to a full black, the probability is that half the offspring will be black and half tabby.

Blue and chocolate-brown cats mated together will produce black kittens. This is because blue and chocolate-brown are dilute forms of black. However, if those kittens are then mated to each other, the next generation may include blacks, blues, chocolates and cats of a lilac colour, if the matings cross a cat carrying two genes for blue with one carrying chocolate.

With the coat colour red, its dilute form cream and the tortoiseshell mixture of red, cream and black, the heredity is complicated by the fact that red can be carried only on an X chromosome so that females with red can be produced only when both parents carry red. Therefore, if a black male is mated to a red female, this could result in red males, tortoiseshell females and, perhaps some black males as well. If the resulting red males and tortoiseshell females are mated, the next generation may contain black males, red males and females and tortoiseshell females. But *no* tortoiseshell males will appear in this or any succeeding generation.

If the original mating is between a black female and a red male, the second generation will be similar to the last example, but with black instead of red females. Similar results also occur when mating blue and cream cats, the dilute forms of red and black. In the first generation of kittens, this mating will produce males of the female colour and female blue-creams. The second generation will produce blue and cream males and cream and blue-cream females where the grandfather was blue. Where the grandfather was cream, the second generation will produce only blue and cream males and blue-cream females. In fact nature does play tricks and the odd tortoiseshell or blue-cream male has occurred. However, they almost inevitably prove to be infertile.

Most cat breeders try to maintain a particular type and will breed like to like, except for such cases as the tortoiseshell where it is not possible. However, a pure strain can sometimes become too extreme with some varieties. Other blood is then introduced to balance it. In seeking to produce a new breed of cat, or in introducing a new colour to a type, it is necessary to cross-breed. Nevertheless, great care is taken to select animals with a known pedigree so that the results can be predicted with some accuracy. The introduction of a wider range of coat colours to breeds, as has happened particularly with the Siamese, has resulted in many pedigree cats which are excellent examples of one coat colour carrying another colour on a recessive gene. This other colour may reappear in their descendants.

Because of their genetic history, some cats can differ from the outward appearance of their parents. However, many kittens do look different from their parents when they are very young. Naturally they all have a characteristic shape common to kittens, but also they all have blue eyes when the lids first open and they acquire their adult eye colour as they grow up. They may also show a tabby pattern which will disappear when they are adult or, in the case of kittens born to Siamese or cats with similar coats, they may at first lack colour markings.

Recognized Breeds

There are now well over 100 breeds and colour varieties of cats recognized by the Governing Council of the Cat Fancy in Britain. If one adds those new breeds seeking recognition and all the breeds and colours accepted in North America, which the British do not have, there is now an extremely wide range of cats. The rest of this book is devoted to a description of the recognized breeds and colour varieties, divided into three broad groups: the short-haired cats which are described on pages 46-71; the long-haired cats on pages 72-97; and the so-called foreign shorthairs on pages 98-121.

No doubt even more variations will be produced from the basic types, colours and patterns that already exist. However many types appear, the similarities between them will be infinitely greater than the outward differences. It is possible to think of some breeds of dog quite separately from each other. For instance, the Irish Wolfhound and the Pug could pass as two species. But a cat, long-haired or Siamese, champion or moggy, will indubitably exhibit a personality, a beauty, a grace and a character which identify them unmistakably as cats.

SHORT-HAIRED CATS

All the wild members of the cat family have short coats and short hair. This also appears to be the normal type for domestic cats, because the genes for short hair are dominant over those for long. Long hair does not persist in feral populations of domestic cats and cats with long fur were apparently unknown in Europe until about 400 years ago. They remained rare for a long time after that. The short-haired cats of Europe provided the original stock for the domestic cats of North America. However, since the development of pedigree breeds, breeders on the opposite sides of the Atlantic Ocean have differed in the characteristics they have preferred. Hence, there are now both British short-hair breeds and American short-hair breeds. The differences between the British and American short-hairs are, however, slight as compared with those between them and some other cats which also owe their origin to the typical European short-hairs of the past.

Another group of short-haired cats have a completely different physique. They are now found in most parts of Europe and North America, but they are generally known as 'foreign' breeds. These cats are described on pages 98-121 of this book.

BRITISH SHORT-HAIR

The British (and European) Short-hair is a sturdy, well-built cat with a rather stocky look. It has a strong-boned skeleton, which is well-upholstered without being fat, and powerfully muscled. Its compact body is only of medium length. Proportionally, the body is rather deep from spine to belly and the chest is broad. The back is carried level and the shortish tail is thick at the base, tapering only slightly to a rounded tip. The legs are short and strong, with rounded paws, and the forelegs should be straight.

The head, which is set on a short, thick neck, is round and massive—almost apple-shaped. The top of the skull should be well-rounded, the

Opposite: Two British Short-hairs: a Silver Tabby Short-hair, left, and a Spotted Tabby, right.

cheeks full, the nose short, broad and straight, and the chin firm. The ears are small and set well apart. They have rounded tips and have a good covering of fur. The eyes are large and round. They are set wide apart and quite level in the face.

The coat of the British Short-hair is short and dense. The fur is fine without either harshness or woolliness, the ideal being plushy-textured. It is not long enough to develop knotty tangles, but it needs regular grooming to remove old hairs, dirt and dust. Hand grooming is effective, but it should not replace regular brushing.

British Short-hairs are recognized in a number of colour varieties, though not in all the cat colour types. There are many mongrel cats which are similar to this short-hair type, but they usually lack the correct combination of fur colour and pattern and

47

eye colour, or they do not match up to the physical characteristics described for the breed.

Pedigree cats are by no means always perfect. Features that could stop a cat from winning prizes in a show include ears that are too pointed or too large; a nose that is too long; deep set or small eyes; eyes that are not of a single colour, such as when there is a tinge of another colour around the rim; a face that is too long and narrow; long legs; or fur that is too open.

BRITISH BLUE

The British Blue is a variety that often exemplifies the British Short-hair type. The coat is often more plush than in other colour varieties and the broad head and short nose often meet the standard more closely than other short-haired cats.

Blue, when used to describe the colour of a cat, is not a bright sky blue but a bluish-grey. Genetically, the colour is actually a dilute form of black. Many years ago, this variety used to be a dark slate blue colour, but a medium to light shade is now required by the standard. It must be an even colour all over, and must not shade from dark to light on different parts of the body. There must be no trace of stripes, bars or other patterning, nor should any white hairs occur in the coat. This cat's large, full eyes should be a rich copper or orange colour. Nose leather and paw pads should match the coat in colour.

The British Blue has a reputation for being a particularly placid and gentle cat. It is usually extremely intelligent.

CHARTREUX

The Chartreux is a French breed. In Britain it is considered synonymous with the British Blue, but some American associations recognize it as a separate variety. The American cat has a broad head with full cheeks, but it is not so round and the ears are perhaps slightly larger and higher set than in the British Blue. The French strain was once more massive than the British and the French standard allows green eyes and a coat of any shade of blue.

British Blue

BLACK SHORT-HAIR

The coat of a Black Short-hair must be completely black without a single white hair, and each hair must be jet black to the roots. Kittens often have a brownish tinge to their fur and show faint tabby markings, but these usually disappear as the kittens grow older. Sometimes, the most un-promising kittens grow up with perfect coats. However, any trace of this 'rustiness' in an adult cat would be a fault. Cats often like to bask in the sun, but too much sun-bathing can produce this rusty tinge and so spoil a pedigree cat's show chances.

The Black Short-hair's physique should conform to the description given above for all British Short-hairs. Its eyes should be deep orange or copper in colour. The nose leather and paw pads should be black.

People once thought that black cats were associated with witchcraft and they were even believed to be one of the forms assumed by the Devil. Hence, in some European countries and in North America, they were often considered to be unlucky.

In Britain, however, they are regarded as symbols of good luck. This is perhaps one reason why black cats are so popular. Although black cats may be common, one that fits the official standard is less frequently encountered. Often their bodies are too sleek. They may also have green instead of orange eyes, large, pointed ears, or a coat that is not pure black.

WHITE SHORT-HAIR

White cats should have coats that are pure white, without any coloured hairs or hint of cream. The nose leather and paw pads are pink. The eyes may either be a deep sapphire blue or a rich gold, orange or copper. In the variety known as 'Odd-eyed' one eye is blue and the other is copper. Because all kittens, whatever their breed, are born with blue eyes, it is impossible to determine the adult eye colour at birth.

White Short-hairs are not albino cats: they are genetically white. When also blue-eyed as adults, they are often deaf. This is not the result of any illness, but it is a disability that

49

is genetically linked with the combination of a white coat and blue eyes. Kittens which have other colours in their ancestry often have a patch of darker fur. This frequently takes the form of a smudge of colour on the top of the head between the ears. This will probably disappear as they grow older. However, this blemish is welcome, because it is a reassuring sign that the kitten's hearing is not affected. Orange-eyed Whites do not have this bias towards deafness, but it is sometimes claimed that Odd-eyed cats may have good hearing on one side while being deaf on the other. White cats also show a greater tendency than other colours to have extra toes. This condition is called *polydactylism*.

White cats are rare in wild or feral populations. Perhaps this is because their coats make them more noticeable, and so they are more vulnerable to predators and more obvious to their own prey. Deafness in the Blue-eyed individuals would also make survival more difficult.

White coats show grease and other stains more than other colours and need more careful grooming. A dusting with talcum powder often helps to absorb grease and dirt. It can then be thoroughly brushed out.

In countries where the black cat was once thought to be unlucky, the white variety was the cat of good omen, but, in Britain, it was linked with bad luck. This superstition now seems to be forgotten, because white cats appear to be popular everywhere nowadays.

Odd-eyed
White Short-hair

Orange-eyed
White Short-hair

Blue-eyed White Short-hair

CREAM SHORT-HAIR

The Cream variety of British Short-hairs should have a light, even-coloured coat that is pale cream, not fawn or orangeish. Cream is genetically a dilute form of red and so when a Cream's colour is too 'hot', it is an indication of the red or tortoise-shell cats from which that Cream was probably derived.

Breeders have had difficulties in producing a variety that showed no trace of darker marking or of any white patches. Indeed, no red variety is recognized in the British Short-hairs because, in the full red, the tabby patterning persists so strongly. Cream kittens with dark markings frequently lose them as they reach maturity, but a spell of extreme weather—hot or cold—can sometimes make them reappear.

This variety must conform to the basic British Short-hair physical type. The eyes should be rich copper- or orange-coloured and the nose leather and paw pads should be red. Old books say that hazel-coloured eyes are permitted, but they have not been allowed in Cream Short-hairs since 1967.

TABBY SHORT-HAIRS

Tabby markings must be the most familiar of all the cat coat patterns. It is the pattern of the wild cat of Europe and it is so dominant that it still shows in the kittens of other varieties that are solid-coloured when adult, and often in the grown cats themselves. The word *tabby* is said to come from the name Attibiya, a district of Baghdad, where a kind of taffeta or watered silk was made. This material gives a good idea of the pattern known as the classic, standard or blotched tabby.

There is also a striped pattern, suggesting the tiger, but this is now officially known as the mackerel pattern. The blotched pattern is thought to have developed from this. Two other patterns are closely linked to the basic tabby: the spotted and agouti-like coat of the Abyssinian. Both are mutations from it. Because both of these patterns are largely confined to separately recognized varieties, they are treated elsewhere (see pages 54 and 100). 'Lined' tabbies with narrow stripes sometimes appear. They are thought to be a half-way stage between the mackerel and the agouti.

The classic tabby pattern is believed to have developed in Europe, where it was already becoming common by the mid-18th century. It spread from Europe, reaching India, for instance, about 100 years later. In Europe, the pattern is now very stable and more frequently encountered than the mackerel pattern. But in eastern countries, it is still variable. Its frequency fluctuates regionally. For instance, the vast majority of tabbies in London are blotched, but this does not hold for the whole of Britain. In Australia classic tabbies still seem to predominate.

Ancient Egyptian tomb paintings and Roman mosaics show mackerel tabbies. They also appear in European paintings by such artists as Pieter Bruegel (1525-1569). But John Aubrey, the English antiquarian, writing in the late 17th century, stated that tabby cats fetched high prices during the reign of Charles I because of their rarity. He called them Cyprus cats. Presumably people then thought that they came from Cyprus.

Today the exact patterning of both the classic and mackerel type is laid down extremely carefully. The classic tabby has three dark stripes running down the back and centred on the spine. Across the shoulders is a pattern shaped like a butterfly with front and hind pairs of wings, with spots within them. On each flank is an oyster-shaped blotch encircled by one or more unbroken rings. The tail is evenly ringed along its length and on the neck and chest are unbroken lines looking like necklaces—the more the better. The legs are evenly barred with bracelets that go all the way from the body markings to the toes. On the face, there are fine pencil markings on the cheeks and an unbroken line running back from the corner of the eye, an M-shaped mark on the forehead and a dark line running over the top of the head. The

belly should be spotted.

The mackerel tabby has the same markings on the head, legs and tail as those of the classic tabby. On the body, there is only a single line running unbroken down the back from the head along the spine to the base of the tail. From this line, narrow lines run at right angles down both sides of the cat.

In both types, the markings are in a darker colour than the body of the coat and are clearly defined. The patches or lines should be continuous and not interrupted or broken up into spots, except on the belly. There must be no white patches, and each of the two colours should be even in shade.

The British Short-hair Tabbies are recognized in three different colour varieties: Silver, Red and Brown.

Silver Tabby
The Silver Tabby has silver fur as the ground colour, with dense black markings in either pattern. The soles of the feet, from toe to heel, are black. The eyes are green or hazel and the paw pads are black. Nose leather should be preferably brick red, but a black nose is permissible.

Red Tabby
The Red Tabby has a coat with a red ground colour and deep rich red markings in either pattern. The lips and chin are red and the sides of the feet dark red. The eyes are a brilliant copper. The nose leather is brick red and the paw pads are deep red.

Brown Tabby
The Brown Tabby has a coat of brilliant, coppery-brown fur, with markings of either pattern in dense black. The backs of the legs from paw to heel are black. The eyes may be orange, hazel or deep yellow in colour. The nose leather is brick red and the paw pads either black or brown.

Brown Tabby

Silver Tabby

Red Tabby

SPOTTED SHORT-HAIR

The Spotted Short-hair was once known as the Spotted Tabby. Its links with the tabby are clear, because it has a strongly contrasting pattern similar to the mackerel tabby, except that the stripes are broken down into spots. A number of spotted cats were apparently around at the end of the 19th century and some even had face markings broken into spots. In the 20th century, however, they were

hardly known until the variety re-appeared in a British show in 1965.

The ideal Spotted Short-hair would have well-balanced, rounded spots. But triangular, star-shaped and ro-sette-like markings are all currently acceptable in the coat. The pattern must not consist of narrow or elon-gated markings which simply look like the broken stripes of a mackerel tabby. The tail should have spotting or broken rings, the legs should be spotted and the face should have typical tabby markings.

The Spotted Short-hair may be any colour of those recognized for cats with fur of all one colour, with appropriate colour spotting and eyes to match. However, it is mainly known in silver with black spots and green or hazel eyes; brown with black spots and orange, hazel or deep yellow eyes; and red with dark red

spots and brilliant copper eyes. The nose leather and paw pads should be of the same colour as in the tabby.

Spotted cats often appear in the native populations of the eastern Mediterranean, but they are usually long-bodied, narrow-headed cats, with long, thin tails of the 'foreign' type. The Spotted Short-hair must conform to the physique require-ments of the British Short-hair, as set out on page 47.

BI-COLOURED SHORT-HAIR

The coat of the Bi-coloured Short-hair is clearly patterned in white and a darker colour. The second colour may be any one of those accepted for cats of all one colour: black, red, blue or even cream. The patches of colour should be evenly distributed, with not more than two-thirds of the coat coloured, nor more than one-half white. The patching should be carried across the face, where a white blaze running from the cat's forehead to the nose is desirable. There should be no sign of ticking or barring on the coloured fur and no stray coloured hairs within the white areas. A symmetrically balanced pattern is preferred. The eyes should be brilliant copper or orange.

BLUE-CREAM SHORT-HAIR

This two-colour variety is not a patched cat. Instead of the clearly defined pattern of the Bi-coloured Short-hair, it has a coat in which the blue and cream fur are softly intermingled. There must *not* be a blaze on the face and, nowhere, especially on the paws, should there be a clear area of fur of unbroken colour. There

Bi-coloured Short-hairs

should be an even balance of blue and cream over the whole coat. Naturally, there should be no tabby markings or patches of white. Eyes are copper or orange, the nose leather blue, and the paw pads blue or pink or a mixture of both. Like all British Short-hairs, this variety has a compact body and a round head with full cheeks.

TORTOISESHELL SHORT-HAIR
Tortoiseshell cats have a three-coloured coat consisting of black

Tortoiseshell Short-hair

56

clearly patched with cream and red on all parts of the body, face, legs, feet and tail. The three colours should be proportionally well-balanced. A cream or red blaze on the face is considered desirable. The eyes are brilliant copper or orange, the nose leather and paw pads being either pink or black or having patches of both colours.

Tortoiseshell cats are nearly always female. When males are born, they are almost all infertile, although two tortoiseshell males were recorded as siring kittens about 80 years ago. To produce tortoiseshells, breeders must mate a tortoiseshell mother with a tom cat that is of good British Short-hair type in one of the accepted colours that make up the tortoiseshell coat. Breeders avoid tabbies, because they are likely to pass on their patterning, which is difficult to eradicate in future generations. The kittens produced may include self-colour blacks and reds as well as tortoiseshells. The tortoiseshell kittens are often very dark-coated when they are born. As they become older,

however, the colours become brighter. Adults with the best markings usually develop from such individuals. Tortoiseshell kittens sometimes occur when an all-black cat and an all-red cat are mated.

TORTOISESHELL AND WHITE SHORT-HAIR

This variety has the three-coloured markings of the Tortoiseshell, combined with a partly white coat. The cheeks, top of the head, ears, back, tail and part of the flanks are covered with a clear, balanced patching of black, red and cream. This colouring should also appear on the paws. The underpart of the body, chest, legs and chin are white and a white blaze on the face is desirable, but tortoiseshell areas must always predominate over the white. The eyes are copper or orange. The nose leather and paw pads are pink or black or they are patched with both colours.

Like the Tortoiseshell, the Tortoiseshell and White Short-hair is basically a female-only variety and the females must be mated to males of other patterns. Although breeding records indicate some unusual sires, including a Blue Long-hair, the obvious choices would be male Bi-coloured or self-coloured of a good type.

Tortoiseshell and White Short-hair

Smoke Short-hair

SMOKE SHORT-HAIR

The coat of the Smoke Short-hair may be either black or blue, with an undercoat of pale silver. When still, these cats look as though they have a solid coat of a dark colour. But the silvery undercoat shines through when they move. The eyes are yellow or orange and the nose leather and paw pads are black or blue to match the colour of the coat.

TIPPED SHORT-HAIR

The British Tipped Short-hair has a white undercoat and topcoat. But each hair on the back, flanks, head, ears and tail is tipped with colour. The tipping is evenly distributed to give a sparkling effect. It may also slightly shade the legs, but the chin, stomach, chest and undertail should be as white as possible. The Tipped Short-hair is recognized in all the colours of short-hair, uniformly coloured cats, and also in brown, chocolate and lilac. In all colours, the nose leather and paw pads should be either pink or correspond to the colour of the tipping as closely as possible. Cats

with black tipping have green eyes. Others have rich orange or copper-coloured eyes.

Tipped Short-hair

This breed was originally created by mating Short-hair Silver Tabbies to Long-hair Chinchillas. The resulting colour variety was a short-haired equivalent to the Chinchilla (see page 82).

AMERICAN SHORT-HAIR

Variously known as the American Short-hair, the Domestic Short-hair and the American Domestic Short-hair, this breed is very similar to the European short-haired cats with which it shares its origins. It was, in fact, developed from cats taken to North America by immigrants from Europe, but there are now distinct differences between the two types.

The American Short-hair is less cobby than the British Short-hair. It has a somewhat longer look, its medium to large body being set on medium-length legs, with firm, rounded paws and heavy pads. The tail is medium-long, heavy at the base like the British cat, and tapering to a blunt end. The neck is of medium length and the head is less round than the British variety, being rather

more heart-shaped. The slightly larger ears are set wide upon the head, but they are less open at the base. The eyes are large, wide-awake and round, with just a hint of a slant at the outer edge. The short, thick fur has a much harder texture than the European Short-hair. American varieties are recognized in a much wider range of coat colours and patterns, although not all of the cat organizations in North America recognize all the varieties of colour and pattern.

WHITE AMERICAN SHORT-HAIR

This variety has a glistening, pure white coat, with pink nose leather and paw pads. It may be blue-, orange- or odd-eyed, like the British White Short-hair (see pages 49-50).

BLACK AMERICAN SHORT-HAIR

This coal black cat with golden eyes is similar to the British Black, except in the ways described above and in that the paw pads may be brown or black.

Red American Short-hair

BLUE AMERICAN SHORT-HAIR

Pale coats are preferred in this colour, but a level tone is more important and a darker cat of an even shade will be preferred to a light-coloured cat of uneven colour. (See also the British Blue, page 48).

RED AMERICAN SHORT-HAIR

A red self-coloured cat is recognized in this breed. In the British type, tabby markings have proved too predominant for it to become an accepted colour. The coat is a deep, rich, brilliant red, with no shading, marking or ticking. The lips and chin are the same colour as the rest of the coat. The nose leather and paw pads are brick red and the eyes are a brilliant gold.

CHINCHILLA AMERICAN SHORT-HAIR

The Chinchilla is the American equivalent of the black variety of the British Tipped Short-hair (page 58). In Britain this is only one of the possible colours of a breed that did not gain recognition until 1978. The

American cat was recognized much earlier.

It has a pure white undercoat and the topcoat is tipped with black on the back, flanks, head and tail, giving a sparkling silver appearance. The chin, stomach and chest must remain pure white, although the legs may be slightly shaded. The rims of the eyes, the lips and the nose are outlined in black, but the nose leather is brick red. The paw pads are black and the eyes a rich emerald or blue-green. (See also Chinchilla Long-hair, page 82).

SHADED SILVER AMERICAN SHORT-HAIR

This cat is a darker version of the Chinchilla in which the tipping on the spine is dark, becoming lighter as it shades to the white underparts. The legs are the same tone as the face.

CAMEO AMERICAN SHORT-HAIR

Shell, Shaded and Smoke Cameos are all recognized in the American Short-hair. The first two are red versions of the Chinchilla and the Shaded Silver, respectively. The Smoke Cameo,

Chinchilla
American
Short-hair

Shaded Silver
American
Short-hair

which is also known as the Red
Smoke, is an even darker red. They
all have rose-coloured nose leather
and pads and brilliant gold eyes.
(See Cameo Long-hairs, page 84).

SMOKE AMERICAN
SHORT-HAIR

The Black Smoke is like the British
cat, apart from following the American
physical type. Its white undercoat is

Shell Cameo
American Short-hair

Smoke Cameo
American
Short-hair

Shaded Cameo
American Short-hair

covered by a jet black coat that gives the cat a solid black appearance except when it is in motion. Nose leather and paw pads are black and the eyes are a brilliant gold. The Blue Smoke has a blue topcoat and blue nose leather and paw pads.

TABBY AMERICAN SHORT-HAIRS
In addition to the Silver, Brown and Red Tabby varieties, which are recognized in the British Short-hair (see pages 51-53), the American Short-hair may also be Blue Tabby, Cream Tabby or Cameo Tabby. The patterns in all cases are like those described for the British Tabby Short-hairs (pages 51-52) but, naturally, they must all conform to the American Short-hair physical type.

The Blue Tabby has a ground colour of pale, bluish-ivory, with contrasting markings in a deep blue. It has brilliant gold eyes, rose paw pads, and 'old rose' nose leather.

The Cream Tabby has a pale cream ground colour to the coat, with darker markings in buff or cream. These markings provide a good contrast, but they remain within a dilute colour range without becoming reddish. It has brilliant gold eyes and pink nose leather and paw pads.

The Cameo Tabby has an off-white ground colour, with red markings, rose nose leather and paw pads, and brilliant gold eyes.

Cameo Tabby
American Short-hair

Cream Tabby
American Short-hair

Blue Tabby
American Short-hair

Calico American Short-hair

Dilute Calico American Short-hair

Blue-cream American Short-hair

PARTI-COLOUR OR BI-COLOUR AMERICAN SHORT-HAIR

This cat is like the British Bi-colour, with patches of solid colour on white. The patches may be black, blue, red or cream. The eye colour in all types is a brilliant gold.

TORTOISESHELL AMERICAN SHORT-HAIR

This is a tri-coloured cat like the British Tortoiseshell Short-hair in colour and pattern (page 56), but it follows the American Short-hair standards in other respects.

TORTOISESHELL AND WHITE AMERICAN SHORT-HAIR

This cat is similar in pattern to the British Tortoiseshell and White Short-hair, but the exact requirements regarding the extent of the white areas of the coat of this variety differ from one American association to another. In some associations, this variety is replaced by the Calico (see below), while some associations recognize both. The eyes are gold.

CALICO AMERICAN SHORT-HAIR

In some American associations, this cat is the equivalent in pattern and colour to the British Tortoiseshell. In others, it is a similar cat, but it has a white coat with tri-colour patches, rather than one divided into coloured and white sections. It can also be a cat with a white ground, patched

only with black and red (no cream). The eyes are gold.

DILUTE CALICO AMERICAN SHORT-HAIR

The dilute form of the Calico is a white cat, patched with unbrindled (clear-coloured) areas of blue and cream. The eyes are brilliant gold.

BLUE-CREAM AMERICAN SHORT-HAIR

The coat on the body, face and extremities of this variety is broken into clearly defined patches of the two colours—the exact opposite of what the British standard requires. The eyes are brilliant gold.

EXOTIC SHORT-HAIR

This variety was created in the United States by crossing American Short-hairs with Persian (Long-hair) cats. This crossing produced a type that had the physique and hair texture of the Persian, but with short fur. It is probably the closest of the American breeds to the British Short-hair, although it is not quite the same.

There is a similarity in that, to re-establish the type in the British cat after the interruption to pedigree breeding during World War II, British breeders also introduced long-hair blood to the British type.

The Exotic has a cobby body, set low on short legs, with a deep chest and equally massive shoulders and rump. The middle section is short and well-rounded. The round and massive head has a broad skull and is set on a short, thick neck. The short tail is usually carried without a curve and at a lower angle than the back. The small, low-set ears are wide apart, tilted forward and round-tipped. The chin is full, as are the cheeks. The nose is short and broad, without a break, and the eyes are large and round. The paws are large and round, with close-set toes. The coat is soft and dense and longer than in the American Short-hair.

It may be solid colour white (odd-eyed, blue-eyed or orange-eyed), black, blue, red or cream; of either mackerel or standard tabby in silver, red, brown, blue, cream or cameo;

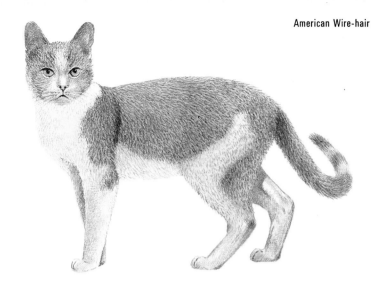

chinchilla, shaded silver, shell or shaded cameo; black, blue or cameo smoke; tortoiseshell, calico, dilute calico, blue-cream or bi-colour. The requirements for coat pattern, eye colour, nose leather and paw pads are the same as for American Short-hairs of the same colour.

AMERICAN WIRE-HAIR

This variety appeared as a natural mutation in a litter of farm cats in New York State. The kitten had a coat like that of a Wire-hair Terrier dog, but it was even coarser and with hair tightly curled on the head and ears. The original cat and its immediate descendants tended to have rather longer legs, heavier hips and shorter heads than the American Short-hair. Breeders now aim for a cat like the American Short-hair in all respects except for the texture of the coat, which should be of medium length and very wiry on the head, back, sides, hips and along the top of the tail. It can be less coarse on the underside of the body and on the chin.

MANX

True Manx cats have no tail, not even the vestige of one. At the end of the spine, where the vertebrae should start to form the tail, they are completely missing and it is possible to feel a hollow at the end of the backbone. This gives the cat a very rounded rump—'round as an orange' is how the British standard used to describe it. The back legs are longer than the short front legs and the hind quarters are carried high, giving an upward slope to the line of the back, although this is often somewhat offset by the bending of the rear legs. In motion the cat seems to have a bobbing, or rather rabbit-like, gait.

In Britain the head should be as near that of the British Short-hair as possible and the nose should be straight. In North America, a definite dip in the nose is preferred by some breeders. The cheeks are prominent. The ears are larger than in the British Short-hair, pointed and set higher on the head. The coat is double, with a thick undercoat and a longer outercoat. Colour and markings follow those permitted for British and American Short-hairs.

All sorts of legends explain how the Manx came to lose its tail. One tells how it was late arriving at the Ark and slipped in just as Noah was shutting the door, trapping its tail and leaving it behind. Another legend relates that it was bitten off by a cat to save her kittens from soldiers who used to kill cats to use their tails as helmet plumes. But taillessness is, of course, a genetic aberration that has been perpetuated. Tailless cats have appeared in various parts of the world, but the name Manx, which refers to the Isle of Man, is significant because an island home is a restricted breeding area. This helped to ensure the recurrence of the type despite the fact that the genetic coding that causes a kitten to be born without a tail is often linked with physical and health problems. Sometimes the reduction of vertebrae is not restricted to the tail and a malfunction of the sphincter muscles is also associated with the malformation. There is a tendency to a high mortality rate and true Manx bred to true Manx through several generations may bear dead kittens. Breeders must be careful to avoid perpetuating such problems.

Even when both Manx parents are completely tailless, some kittens in the litter will probably have tails, either complete or reduced in length. 'Stumpy' (short-tailed) and Tailed Manx are now recognized as British varieties. Some American organizations recognize five different stages from the tailless to the completely tailed. The stages are called Rumpy (tailless), Riser (with a small number of vertebrae which can be felt or seen), Stubby (with a distinct and moveable short tail), Longy (with a longer but not a full-length tail), and Tailed.

Manx may be any colour or pattern, with eyes matching the coat as described for other colour varieties.

BOMBAY

This American variety was created by breeding a Black American Short-hair to a Burmese. This produced a cat with the colour and type of the Short-hair and the sleek coat of the Burmese. The head is round with a full face and considerable breadth between the eyes, tapering, with a definite nose break, to a short, well-developed muzzle. The large, round eyes are yellow to deep copper in colour, the darker the better. The

Bombay

Manx

Rumpy (tailless)

Longy (longer tail)

Stumpy (short tail)

67

body is neither cobby nor rangy and the tail is straight and of medium length. The short, close-lying coat has a fine, satin-like texture and a sheen like patent leather, a feature particular to this variety.

SCOTTISH FOLD

The Scottish Fold is a variety of cat with dropped ears. It developed from a chance mutation which appeared in Perthshire, Scotland, in 1961. Its development has caused much controversy among cat lovers. It is not accepted as a breed in Britain, although a Fold kitten won a prize in a British show in 1971. However, the judges considered the kitten to be a normal prick-eared cat, because its ears had not, at that stage, developed the characteristic droop. In North America, the type has gained favour with some breeders and has been accepted as a registered variety by some organizations.

Because the original mutant was bred to British Short-hairs, the cat is of basic British Short-hair type. It is cobby-bodied and round-headed, with a short neck. Its coat is short and soft. The ears are usually small and they fold forward and down at the top of the ear pocket, making it difficult to clean them properly. The fold may be only slight in kittens, but there must be a definite fold line in adults.

In North America, the Scottish Fold is accepted in the following colours: white, black, blue, red, cream and cameo; chinchilla, shaded silver, shaded and shell cameo; black, blue and cameo smoke; tortoiseshell, calico, dilute calico, blue-cream and bi-colour. The eyes and leather should be the same as for short-haired cats of the same coat colour and pattern.

In other species, drop-ears appear only after many centuries of domestication. There are reports of drop-eared cats in old books. One late 18th-century publication reported that they were common in China. Around 80 years ago, a sailor brought home a drop-eared cat which he claimed had come from China. There, he said, the breed was raised for food. Not until 1938 was another such cat reliably reported and then, 23 years later, the Perthshire mutant appeared.

Are drop-ears so uncharacteristic of cats that they will always seem

odd? Or will they eventually become as acceptable as they are in some types of dogs and goats? Before making up one's mind about this variety, it would be interesting to see a scientific assessment of any effect of drop-ears on the cats' hearing and susceptibility to ear infections.

REX

Rex cats are another comparatively recent development. They result from a natural mutation which affects the cat's coat and which also occurs occasionally in other animals, including rabbits.

The fur of most cats is made up of several kinds of hair. There are long, straight, thick hairs which taper evenly; curving hairs which thicken and then taper suddenly; crimped hairs which are somewhere between the other two; and down hairs which are evenly thin and crimped.

In most cats, there are 50 times as many of the last type of hairs as there are of the first. But, in the Rex cat's coat, the fur consists almost entirely of down hairs or, in one type, of down hairs plus a small proportion of the third type of crimped hair. The length of individual hairs is only about half

that of the fur of normal short-haired cats and its thickness is reduced by more than a third. The result is a short, plushy coat with a rippling waved effect, which is especially noticeable on the back. The whiskers and eyebrows are crinkly.

The first cat known to have this kind of coat was born in Germany in the 1940s. In the 1950s this cat produced kittens in East Berlin. Imported into the United States, these kittens played a part in the development of the North American Rex variety. There were also two isolated mutations in the United States: one in Ohio in 1953 and another in Oregon in 1959. But, by then, breeding had already begun from Rex cats imported from Britain.

The British Rex strains have their origins in a cat with Rex-type fur born to a Cornish farm cat in 1950 and a cat born in neighbouring Devon ten years later. In Britain, they are recognized as two separate varieties.

CORNISH REX

One kitten in an otherwise normal litter, born of an unknown father to a Tortoiseshell and White cat in Bodmin, Cornwall, had a curly coat.

About half of its own offspring had curly coats. Although deriving from ordinary short-haired cats, the Rex has a longer, slimmer body, more like that of the Siamese and other cats of the foreign type. It has long, straight legs, small oval paws and a long, tapering tail. The head is slightly wedge-shaped and the ears are large and high set, with rounded tips. The coat may be any colour. If there are any white markings, they must be symmetrical, except in tortoiseshell and white. The ears and tail should carry plenty of fur. The eyes are oval and should be coloured as appropriate to the coat. Cornish and German Rex have the same genetic coding and, when mated, can produce Rex-type kittens.

DEVON REX

This variety, although it has a similar coat, is produced by a different set of genes. When mated with Cornish or German Rex, only plain-coated litters are produced, although second-generation matings from those cats will produce Rex-type kittens.

The Devon Rex has a broader chest and shorter neck than the Cornish type. Its head looks quite different, with full cheeks and a distinct break in the nose. The muzzle is short with a strong chin and the whisker pads are noticeable. The eyes are large and slightly oval and the large ears are set low on the head. All colours except bi-colours are acceptable. White markings are considered a fault except in cats which are tortoiseshell and white. The eye colour should be in keeping with the coat and (except in the Si-Rex) chartreuse, green or yellow. The Si-Rex simply shows the point pattern of the Siamese and is not a separate variety. It has blue eyes.

SPHYNX

The Sphynx is a variety, not recognized in Britain nor by several of the American cat associations, which has been developed from a chance mutation which appeared in a litter born in Ontario, Canada, in 1966. The mother was a black and white domestic pet and her kittens were quite normal except for one which had no hair!

Hairless cats have appeared before in other places. Among them were a

Devon Rex

pair of Siamese born in France and another pair in London. In fact, none were completely hairless, except at birth.

The Sphynx has a covering of soft, downy hair. This hair is hardly perceptible except on the large ears, the muzzle, tail, feet and the testicles of the males, where it is tightly packed and more noticeable. There may also be a ridge of short, wiry hair down the spine and the face is covered with a soft pile. Eyebrows and whiskers are lacking. The cat's coat feels like suede to the touch.

Although not developed from oriental-looking cats, the Sphynx, like the Rex and the only two similar British cats the author has seen, has the long body, long, tapering tail, neat, oval feet and more wedge-shaped head of the foreign type. The mutation of the fur appears to be connected with an overall change in physique.

Sphynx breeders say that these cats prefer people to other cats. But they do not like being cuddled, although they will settle on a friendly lap, sometimes standing with one front paw lifted, a typical stance for this variety.

Sphynx have a high body temperature. They sweat and, without a coat to retain their heat, they like a warm environment. When it is cold, they will snuggle up against a heat source even more than other cats, but they are not frail cats and should be strong and muscular.

The skin of adults should be taut and wrinkle-free, except for the head, although kittens often look as though they have a skin several times too large for them, because it is loose and puckered. The rather barrel-shaped chest of the Sphynx encourages a slightly bow-legged look, which is particularly noticeable in kittens. Except for its sloping eyes, the cat looks from the front a little like a Boston Terrier dog. The Sphynx coat may be in any of the colours accepted for short-haired cats.

LONG-HAIRED CATS

Some wild members of the cat family, such as the Northern Lynx and the Snow Leopard, have slightly longer hair than others. However, none has truly long hair as we know it in some of our domestic cats. Genetically, long hair is recessive to short hair and, in the absence of man, it creates various problems. For instance, while grooming itself, a long-haired cat will swallow more fur and this can lead to the development of fur balls and internal blockages. Grooming long fur is also more difficult, because it tangles and holds dirt. Wounds are less easy to keep clean and parasites more difficult to dislodge. For these reasons, a domestic long-hair needs regular brushing and grooming by its owner.

No evidence of long-haired cats exists in the literature or art of ancient times. The first ones known to Europeans appear to have been seen in the Middle East. Travellers took them home as a curiosity. They were introduced into Italy in about 1550 and they were known in France before the end of the 16th century, but they remained rare for a long time. If allowed freedom to roam, they would have mated with short-hairs and, because long hair is recessive, the chances of their descendants being long-haired were slight. There also seems to have been little thought of deliberately breeding a strain of long-haired cats in the West until about 130 years ago.

It is generally thought that the earliest long-haired cats were probably like modern Angora cats and came from Turkey. However, by the mid-19th century, when people were beginning to be enthusiastic about particular kinds of cat and were consciously breeding them, a heavier type was more popular. This was generally known as the Persian. It was probably taken to Europe from what is now Iran, although its true origin may have been much farther away to the east. It is not quite the cat that we now know as the Persian, because this modern cat shows the effects of 100 years or so of controlled breeding to produce kittens to match peoples' tastes. Cat fanciers towards the end of the 19th century were more enthusiastic about long-haired cats than about their more common short-haired pets and they had definite ideas about the kind of appearance that they should have. Their breeding programme produced a cat which, in Britain, is now officially known simply as the Long-hair. But this cat is still called the Persian by most of the North American cat associations and is often still talked of as the Persian even in Britain.

Opposite: A Chinchilla Long-hair, or Chinchilla Persian, with its darkly-outlined eyes, can be one of the most beautiful of long-haired cats.

Angora

ANGORA

Angora cats got their name from the Turkish city of Angora, which we now call Ankara. Their silky fur is like that of the Angora goat (mohair), which comes from the same area, and the Angora rabbit was so named because of its similar coat. Although Angoras were probably the first long-hairs in Europe, interest passed to the heavier Persian cat in the last quarter of the 19th century and, in Turkey itself, the Angora almost disappeared. It was saved from extinction by a specially organized breeding programme at Ankara Zoo.

In 1963 permission was given for a pair of Angora cats to be taken from Ankara to the United States. Three years later, another pair were also exported. The breed was re-established in the United States from these four cats. Angoras are now being bred in Britain but they are not sufficiently widespread there for them to be recognized as a breed.

The Angora has a longish body and tail and a small, neat head, with large, upright ears. The eyes are large and almond-shaped, with a slight slope upwards. The legs are long, with small, round, dainty paws. The back legs are longer than the front legs,

so that the rump is carried slightly higher than the rest of the back. The tail is long and tapering. When the cat is on the move, the tail is often carried forward horizontally over the back. The medium-length coat tends to waviness, especially on the stomach. There are tufts of hair between the toes and at the ear tips. There is also a good furnishing of hair in the ears.

The Angoras bred at Ankara Zoo are all white cats and this is now the accepted colour for the variety. Eyes may be blue, amber or one of each colour. White, blue-eyed cats may be deaf, as in other varieties (see page 76). The paw pads, lips and nose leather should be pink. In the past, the Angora was known in black, blue and other colours, and may be so again. This affectionate cat is said to be adept at learning tricks.

LONG-HAIR (PERSIAN)

The basic long-hair type recognized in Britain and the American Persian are the same variety. However, as with all types of cat, individual breeders or show judges may prefer a different emphasis in what they consider to be the perfect type. The cat has a short, cobby body (massive and low-lying), with a level back, a deep chest, a short and powerful neck and a massive head. The legs are short and thick. The toes are set close together in the large, round feet. The tail is short, but it is in proportion to the body and does not taper. The head is round and broad, with full cheeks and a short nose. American standards specify that there shall be a definite break, or stop, where the nose meets the forehead. The eyes are large and round. The ears are small, set far apart and low on the head. They are not very open at the base, tilt forward slightly and have rounded tips. The Long-hair's coat is luxuriant and flowing. There is a full ruff around the neck and over the top of the chest, a sumptuous tail and long tufts on the ears and between the toes.

Long-hairs are recognized in a wide range of colour varieties in Britain and the equivalent Persian in North America is known in even more colours. In most cases the requirements in a cat of show standard are the same on both sides of the Atlantic, but there are occasional differences.

BLACK LONG-HAIR (BLACK PERSIAN)

The Black Long-hair should have an absolutely pure black coat, but perfect specimens are not common. Even a single white hair will show clearly against the raven black coat. A slight rustiness may also show up in the fur in certain lights, especially when the cat is moulting or if it has been basking in sunshine for long periods. Owners are advised, after brushing and grooming, to rub the fur with a piece of silk or chamois leather in the direction of the lie of the coat. This final touch will give the cat an extra, glossy sheen. It will also help to remove any stray white hairs which tend to be of a coarser texture than the rest of the fur. Black Long-hairs should have the shape and build of their type. The jet black fur should be matched with black nose leather and paw pads, and the large eyes should be copper or deep orange.

Black Long-hair

WHITE LONG-HAIR (WHITE PERSIAN)

Like its short-haired counterpart, this variety may have either blue eyes, orange eyes, or one eye orange and one blue, the colours being rich and brilliant. Originally, only the blue-eyed type was known. However, this White had perhaps more Angoran ancestry than other Persians and Blue Long-hair blood was introduced to improve the long-hair appearance of the cat. This crossing brought in the orange eye colour and odd eyes. Because of this background of crossings, a mating between cats of the same eye colour often produces a litter including kittens with any of the three types. The linking of the white coat and blue eyes carries an hereditary tendency to deafness. However, a kitten which has any dark patch of fur is not usually deaf, even though the patch will disappear as the cat matures.

The White Long-hair should have a pure white coat, without any mark or blemish. Its nose leather and paw pads should be pink.

BLUE LONG-HAIR (BLUE PERSIAN)

The British standard for this variety allows the coat to be any shade of blue, provided that it is even in colour and free from any marking or white hairs. Lighter shades are definitely preferred in North America, although evenness of colour is more important than its strength. The Blue Long-hair's eyes are deep, brilliant copper or orange. Nose leather and paw pads are blue. This variety has a particularly full ruff around the neck and over the chest. Some of the finest-looking adults develop from kittens which have clearly visible, shadowy, tabby markings.

RED LONG-HAIR (RED PERSIAN)

Long-hairs with all red fur are recognized on both sides of the Atlantic. Solid red, or red self, cats have been developed from Red Tabbies. The tabby markings which persist so strongly in short-haired red cats are not so noticeable in long-haired cats, although it is rare to find them completely lacking, especially from the face. Kittens which are strongly marked at birth may take 18 months to two years to get their final coat, so there is plenty of time for the pattern to fade. In the past this variety has been known as an orange

White Long-hair

Blue Long-hair

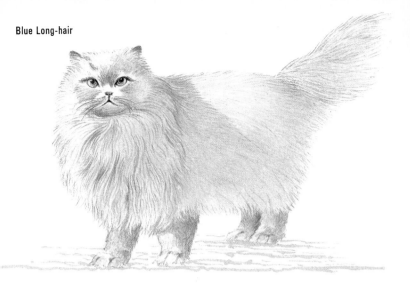

or a marmalade cat, but the colour should be truly red, although at the orange end of the red range.

The lips and chin should be the same colour as the coat, not white or cream as is often the case. The whiskers should also be red. The eye colour is deep, brilliant copper. The nose leather and paw pads are brick red. Red coloration is caused by a gene which appears to be sex-linked, and, because red females are comparatively rare, crossings with Black and Tortoiseshell cats have been used to produce solid Reds.

CREAM LONG-HAIR (CREAM PERSIAN)

The cream coat colour is created by the combination of the genetic coding

Red Long-hair

for both red and for a dilution of colour. This variety owes its development possibly to both the offspring of very pale Reds and to matings between Red and Blue Long-hairs. Some early cats of this variety were fawn in colour, but a paler shade is now expected. Because the red element is sex-linked, cream females are produced only when cream is mated to cream, or in pairings where both parents carry both red and dilution factors. Eyes in the Cream Long-hair must be a rich copper colour. The nose leather and paw pads are pink.

TABBY LONG-HAIR (TABBY PERSIAN)

Tabby long-haired cats may have either the classic or the mackerel type tabby markings (see page 51). In either case the markings must be clearly defined, although long fur tends to make their edges softer than in short-haired cats, and the strength of contrast between ground and pattern varies from colour to colour.

Silver Tabby Long-hair (Silver Tabby Persian)

This is a truly beautiful cat, although Silver Tabbies may not always satisfy those who like an extreme Persian-type head. This is because the nose and face tend to be less flattened than in some other varieties. The pattern of lustrous black on a silver ground, matched to bright green or hazel eyes with red nose leather, will always win admirers. The paw pads are black.

Many of the most attractive Silver Tabbies are extremely dark at birth, almost solid black except on the legs and sides. The markings begin to separate from the coat as the kitten grows and may not be complete until it is about six months old.

Brown Tabby Long-hair (Brown Tabby Persian)

The British standard for this variety describes a pattern with the butterfly wings outlined across the shoulders and deep bands running down the saddle and sides. There is no mention of the usual whorls of the classic pattern, nor of the mackerel type. However, the two usual patterns are both recognized as separate varieties and, in practice, are accepted in Britain. The coat should be a rich tawny brown, with clear black markings. There is often a tendency to lighter, or even white patches on

Silver Tabby Long-hair

Brown Tabby Long-hair

Red Tabby Long-hair

Blue Tabby Persian

Cream Tabby Persian

Cameo Tabby Persian

the chin and around the lips, but this is a definite fault. The eyes are copper or hazel in colour. The nose leather is red and the paw pads are either black or brown.

Red Tabby Long-hair (Red Tabby Persian)

The Red Tabby's coat should be a rich red, with markings boldly defined in an even darker red. The eyes are deep copper in colour. The nose leather is brick red and the paw pads are pink.

Cream Tabby Persian

The British Cat Fancy does not yet recognize a Cream Tabby Long-hair, but it is accepted in North America. The ground colour, including the lips and chin, is a pale cream. The markings are in buff or a cream sufficiently darker than the body of the coat to give a good contrast. The eyes are bright copper or gold and the nose leather and paw pads are pink.

Blue Tabby Persian

The Blue Tabby is another variety recognized in North America but not in Britain. The ground colour is a pale, bluish-ivory, including lips and chin, with deep blue markings. The whole is permeated with a warm fawn overtone. The eyes are brilliant copper or gold. The nose leather is old rose and the paw pads are rose. This colouring has occurred spontaneously in litters of brown tabbies. It can also be produced by mating Brown Tabbies to solid Blues.

Cameo Tabby Persian

The Cameo Tabby is another colouring recognized in North America, but not in Britain. The Cameo Tabby has an off-white ground colour, with red markings. The eyes are bright copper or gold. The nose leather and paw pads are rose.

PEKE-FACED PERSIAN

This is a variety which has been known in North America for nearly 50 years, but the British Cat Fancy has not approved it. The Peke-faced Persian's coat may be either red-tabby or solid-red.

The variety follows the usual Persian type, looking very like other Persian cats except for its face. This has a pushed-in frontal look, with a retroussé (upturned) nose, and heavy wrinkles on the muzzle and from the

Peke-faced Persian

81

Shaded Silver
Persian

Chinchilla
Long-hair

corners of the eye. The eyes are large and round and somewhat protrusive. As the name of the variety suggests, it closely resembles a Pekinese dog. While these cats can have considerable charm and personality, they are similar to Pekinese, Pugs and other dogs with flattened faces, in that they risk developing breathing problems because of their extremely short noses. The fold of skin beneath the eyes can sometimes cause the tear ducts to become blocked. Another danger is that the teeth of the upper jaw do not meet correctly with those of the lower jaw.

Breeders must be extremely careful not to perpetuate any deformity that is harmful to the animal. This problem is inherent in aiming for such an extreme appearance, so unlike the original feline type. Some kittens display the characteristic break between the nose and the forehead within a day or so of their birth. Others do not develop it for up to six months.

CHINCHILLA LONG-HAIR (CHINCHILLA PERSIAN)

The Chinchilla's pure white under-coat, topped by a long, silky fur which is tipped with black on the back, flanks, tail, head and ears, makes it an especially striking cat. It is also known in the United States as the Silver Persian.

In Britain it is accepted that this is usually a smaller and more dainty looking cat than the other varieties of the long-hairs. In North America, however, it is expected to be of full Persian type. The emerald or blue-green eyes, which are heavily outlined by dark rims of black skin on the edges of the eyelids, and the brick red of the nose leather enhance the effect. The paw pads are black.

It is said that the Chinchilla was created in Britain in the 1880s when a breeder crossed a Silver Tabby Long-hair with a Smoke Long-hair and the earlier version of the breed was much darker than the modern cat. Chinchilla kittens are nearly

Blue-smoke Long-hair

Smoke Long-hair

always born with quite dark fur and noticeable tabby markings, especially on the tail, which disappear as they grow older.

SHADED SILVER PERSIAN

If one thinks of the Chinchilla as the Silver Persian, then the Shaded Silver Persian might aptly be called the Pewter Persian. It is exactly like a Chinchilla except that the tipping of its fur is heavier, giving it a much darker overall look. The shading should grade evenly from dark on the spine to white on the chin, chest and stomach, with the legs matching the face in tone.

Both Chinchillas and Shaded Silvers can be born in the same litter and it is not possible to tell the variety of the youngest kittens, because the darkest ones sometimes mature to have the lightest coats. In Britain it was found to be extremely difficult to decide the variety of even an adult cat. In 1902, therefore, it was decided to drop the Shaded Silver

category, but it is still considered a separate variety in North America and Australia. Like the Chinchilla, the eyes are deep green or blue-green, the nose leather is brick red and the paw pads are black.

SMOKE LONG-HAIR (SMOKE PERSIAN)

The Smoke Long-hair may have derived from crossings between Blacks and Whites and other long-haired cats. It has a white undercoat, while the uppercoat is heavily tipped with black. The tipping is darkest on the back, head and feet and shades to silver on the sides. When the cat is still, the general effect is of a black cat. When it moves, the white undercoat shows through clearly. The fur on the feet and the face is black except at the very base of each hair, where there is a narrow band of white. The generous ruff and ear tufts look silver. The eyes are brilliant copper or orange. The nose leather and the paw pads are black.

Shaded Cameo
Persian

Smoke Cameo
Persian

Shell Cameo
Persian

BLUE SMOKE LONG-HAIR
(BLUE SMOKE PERSIAN)
The Blue Smoke is identical to the Black Long-hair in all save the colour of the coat, which is deeply tipped with blue, and the nose leather and paw pads which should also be blue. The eyes are copper or orange.

SHELL CAMEO PERSIAN
This variety is a red version of the Chinchilla, produced by crossing Chinchillas and solid Reds. They have been recognized for 20 years in the United States. However, they still await breed status in Britain,

although they have been seen for many years. The American standard describes the undercoat as ivory white. British breeders aim at a colour from off-white to a light cream. The uppercoat is very lightly tipped with red, making this a cat with no more than a pink blush to its coat. British breeders will also accept cream tipping, but this is not permitted in North America. The top of the head, ears, back and the upper-side of the tail should all be lightly tipped, shading to a totally untipped chin, chest, stomach and underside to the tail. The ear tufts are untipped, but the face and legs may be lightly tipped. The large, copper-coloured eyes are outlined by rose-coloured rims to the upper and lower eyelids. The nose leather and paw pads are also rose.

SHADED CAMEO PERSIAN

This cat is a slightly darker form of the Shell Cameo, to which it is identical in all respects other than the depth of the colour.

SMOKE CAMEO PERSIAN

Also known as the Red Smoke, this cat, the darkest version of the Cameo, is indeed the red equivalent of the other Smoke varieties. Various bodies specify slightly different shades for the undercoat from white or ivory to cream. The uppercoat is so heavily tipped with red that the cat appears to be solid red in repose. The pale undercoat is revealed only when it moves. This variety is like the other smokes in all respects except colour, with red substituted for blue or black in the coat, and the nose leather, eye rims and paw pads being of a rose colour.

BI-COLOUR LONG-HAIR (PARTI-COLOURED PERSIAN)

The British standard for this variety

Bi-colour Long-hairs

85

American Blue-cream
Long-hair

British Blue-cream
Long-hair

allows the coat to be any solid colour and white. In North America, however, where it is also known as the Parti-coloured Persian, it is restricted to white with either black, blue, red or cream. The patching of the long, silky coat should be clearly defined and the patches of colour should extend over the face. A white blaze between the nose and forehead, or as an inverted V over the face, is particularly liked. The large, round eyes should be deep orange or brilliant copper in colour. The nose leather and paw pads should be in accordance with the coat colours.

BLUE-CREAM LONG-HAIR (BLUE-CREAM PERSIAN)

In North America the Blue-Cream variety is like a Parti-coloured cat. Its coat is patched distinctly with the two colours. In Britain, on the other hand, the colours should merge and intermingle to give an effect somewhat like shot silk. American breeders like to see a cream blaze running down from the forehead. Eyes should be deep copper or dark orange in colour. Both Blue and Cream are dilute forms (of black and red). Most Blue-Creams are female and no record exists of successful mating from a Blue-Cream male. Blue-Creams are occasionally born to Tortoiseshell mothers and such cats are, in effect, dilute forms of tortoiseshell. More frequently, however, Blue-Creams are born to Blue and Cream crosses. In such crosses, breeders avoid the risk that red colouring from the Tortoiseshell will persist.

TORTOISESHELL LONG-HAIR (TORTOISESHELL PERSIAN)

The three colours which make up the tortoiseshell coat, red, cream and black, should be evenly distributed and well-broken into patches on the body, face, legs and feet. A cream or red blaze from the nose to forehead is considered an enhancement. Black must never be the dominant colour in the coat. It is more difficult to obtain clearly defined areas of the three colours in a long-hair and the hard-edged patches of short-haired cats should not be expected.

The eyes should be copper or deep orange. The nose leather and paw pads should be tri-coloured like the coat.

This is another variety in which like-to-like matings are not possible. A Black or Cream male is often used, or a solid-red if one with an unmarked coat is available. Red Tabbies should be avoided, because the offspring would probably carry the tabby pattern. Litters will contain a mixture of colours. Depending on the colour of the stud cat, the kittens may be cream, black, blue-cream or red. There is no guarantee that a litter will include a single tortoiseshell.

TORTOISESHELL AND WHITE LONG-HAIR (TORTOISESHELL AND WHITE PERSIAN)

In Britain the wording of the standard for Tortoiseshell and White Long-hairs describes a coat that is slightly different from that of the Tortoiseshell and White Short-hair. It states that the three-colour patching shall be broken and interspersed with white, rather than requiring the colours to be mainly on the back and upperpart of the cat and the white below. However, there must still be a good balance between the colours and white, which must not be too dominant.

Some American standards specify a pattern more like the short-hair with white legs, feet and underparts, extending halfway up the body, and with white splashes on the nose and half way around the neck. The eyes should be deep orange or brilliant copper. The nose leather and paw pads should have broken colour, like

Tortoiseshell
Long-hair

the coat. In some American associations, the Calico is the same as the British Tortoiseshell and White. Males are extremely rare.

CALICO PERSIAN

This North American variety may be either a cat with a white ground coat patched with red and black, or a white cat patched with red, black and cream. Its belly should be white and there should be predominantly white areas on the chest, legs, paws and face, preferably including a white blaze. The variety sometimes forms the American equivalent of the Tortoiseshell and White Long-hair. In other associations, it exists as a distinct variety alongside it. The Calico will usually carry more white in the coat than the Tortoiseshell and White. Male Calico cats are extremely rare and usually sterile.

DILUTE CALICO PERSIAN

This cat is similar to the Calico, except that its patching is of blue and cream on white (blue and cream being the dilute forms of black and red). White should predominate on the underparts. The eyes are brilliant copper.

MAINE COON CAT

This personable American variety of cat got its name partly from the eastern seaboard state of Maine and partly from a belief that it derived from a cross between a raccoon and a domestic cat. Such a mating could not possibly produce kittens and can be ruled out.

Maine Coon Cats have been around for a long time. They were popular in the second half of the 19th century, but were then ignored until interest in the variety revived in the 1950s. Their appearance gives an

Tortoiseshell and White Long-hair

Calico Persian

Dilute Calico Persian

Maine Coon Cat

immediate clue to their probable ancestry. They have characteristics of both the American Domestic Short-hair and the Angora and are probably the result of cross-breeding between short-haired cats, brought by early European settlers, and Angoras, brought home by sailors on later voyages. These cats are thought to have been feral and free-roaming in the New England countryside.

Maine Coon Cats certainly lack the cobby, short-bodied, low-slung look of the Persian and their fur is not so long. Although they are often large cats, some weighing as much as 13.5 kg (30 lb), they have quite delicate-looking faces, with high cheek bones, large upright, pointed ears, slightly slanting, oval eyes and a long nose, with little or no break. The neck, body and tail are all long, and these strong and sturdy cats have powerful muscles and substantial legs.

Surviving in the countryside through rigorous Maine winters, this cat has developed a rugged coat. Its fur is not as long as the Persian's, but it is quite heavy. It is relatively short on the shoulders, becoming gradually longer towards the tail and ending in shaggy, heavy breeches around the flanks. It gets gradually longer at the sides towards the stomach. The fur on the tail is long and full. There is a frontal ruff beginning at the base of the ears and the ears themselves are well tufted. There is little undercoat and this makes the cat easy to groom. Its fur rarely gets badly tangled.

The Maine Coon Cat can have a wide range of coat colours and patterns: white, black, blue, cream, all colours and types of tabby, tortoiseshell, tortoiseshell and white, calico, blue-cream and bi-colour. It may also be tabby and white, a coat not recognized in either American or British Short-hairs or in Persian cats. The eye colour may be shades of green, gold or copper. The colours do not have to agree with the coat colour as laid down for other varieties. White-coated cats may also have blue eyes or odd-coloured eyes. The nose leather and paw pads should match the coat.

COLOURPOINT (HIMALAYAN)

The Colourpoint Cat is of the Persian type, but it has the coat pattern and colours of the Siamese. In North America, it is called Himalayan. The term Colorpoint is used to describe another variety (page 110).

If long-haired cats are mated directly to Siamese, the kittens which result are not like either parent. The dominant genetic coding produces short-haired, solid-coloured coats, but the recessive genes for long hair and the 'point' pattern of the Siamese (see page 103) are not lost. They reappear in subsequent matings. Among the grandkittens of the original pairing, one in about 16 has long fur and Siamese markings. These cats are unlikely to have the cobby look and correct physique of the Persian type of long-hair. To achieve that, they are bred again to other long-haired cats, the method used in Britain to develop the variety. Alternatively, the method usually used in North America is to breed those kittens that are closest to a Persian look with each other until a Persian type cat results.

Attempts to create a cat of this type were made before World War II in Sweden, North America and Britain. At that time, they met with little success, although some long-haired Siamese were produced. It was not until the late 1940s that the new variety began to appear. It was sufficiently established in Britain to gain recognition in 1955 and, because Black and Blue Long-hairs had featured strongly in the breeding programme, Seal and Blue were the first colours to be recognized. American associations began to grant recognition two years later, but under the name Himalayan.

This cat has a low, cobby body on short but sturdy legs, small, low-set ears, a short nose and full cheeks, and round eyes as close as possible to the Long-hair (Persian) type. The eyes are always brilliant blue. The coat is long, thick and soft in texture and there is a full frill over the neck and chest. The tail is luxuriant. There are long tufts at the ears.

Colour and pattern follow those of the Siamese, with face mask, ears, legs and feet and tail of a darker coloured fur, set off against a pale body colour. In addition to the original seal and blue, there are now a number of other colours. Those recognized in Britain are chocolate, lilac, red, tortie (tortoiseshell) and cream, all of which are Siamese colours, and a blue-cream, chocolate-cream and lilac-cream, which are not accepted in the Siamese. In North America, there are even more colours, because the Tortie may be seal, cream, blue or lilac, each combined with red and/or cream. They may also be red, lilac, chocolate or seal lynxpoint (like the Lynx or Tabby-point Siamese).

BIRMAN

The Birman is another long-haired cat with a pattern of darker points like that of a Siamese, although the Birman has white paws. It is not of the Persian type and it does not have the usual long-hair type in its ancestry. It is said to be a variety first known in Burma and to have links with Tibet and Kampuchea. The Birman was first known in the West when a pregnant female was taken to France. There it became known as *le Chat Sacré de Birmanie*, meaning 'the Sacred Cat of Burma'.

A legend explains this name. It tells of a white cat which lived in the temple of the goddess Tsun-Kyan-Kse at Lao-Tsun. It was one of several white cats kept by the priests, who believed that the spirits of the dead lived on in them. One night the temple was attacked and, either just before or during the fighting (versions differ), the chief priest was killed. As he died, the cat stood upon his head

Colourpoints
(Himalayans)

and faced the goddess. As the priest's spirit entered the cat, the animal's coat took on the golden glow of the goddess, its eyes become the sapphire blue of her eyes, its legs became brown like the earth from which all life springs, and its feet kept the whiteness of the priest's hair, a symbol of purity. Inspired by this miracle, the other priests were filled with confidence and courage and defeated their attackers. Next morning they found that all the temple's cats had changed to the same colours and pattern and they persisted in their descendants.

Two of these Burmese cats were sent as a gift to France in 1919 by Burmese, who were grateful for French help at a later stage in the temple's history. One cat died on the journey. The other was the pregnant female mentioned above and it is from her that the Western strain has derived.

In North America the 'golden' colouring is seen today as a pale fawn to cream in the Seal variety of the Birman, although it is claimed that cats with pure blood-lines from the original strain have a golden halo to the whole back of the coat. A golden look is certainly expected in Europe. The British standard describes the coat as beige that is slightly golden. It has coloured points and mask like the Siamese, but the paws look as though the cat has walked into a saucer of milk. The white 'gloves', as they are called, extend to an even line across the paw at the third joint and up the back of

Blue Point Birman

Seal Point Birman

the hind legs to end in a point. The white areas on the back of the legs are known as the 'laces'.

The Birman has a long but fairly stocky body. The head is broad and rounded, unlike either the Siamese or the Persian, because it has a nose of medium length. The ears are larger than the Persian's and both the tail and legs are longer. The fur is long and silky in texture and tends to curl on the stomach. There is a ruff around the neck. The medium-length tail has a plume of long, silky fur, unlike the bouffant Persian.

The original variety of Birman, as the legend of its colouring describes, was the Seal variety with a beige coat, seal-brown points and nose leather, pink paw pads (again unlike the Siamese), white 'gloves' and

bright blue eyes. The Blue Point came next. It has a bluish white body colour, shading almost to white on the stomach and chest and with deep blue points. The nose leather is slate grey, the paw pads are pink and the eyes are blue. Chocolate and Lilac Point Birmans are also recognized in North America. Their colouring follows that described for the Siamese (see page 106).

SOMALI

This variety is a long-haired version of the Abyssinian Cat (see page 100). It has not yet achieved recognition in Britain. It first appeared as a natural long-haired mutation probably in Canada, but also in the United States and Europe.

It has exactly the same physique as

Ruddy Somali

Red Somali

93

Ragdolls

the Abyssinian. The body is long and lithe and the tail is thick-based and tapering. The head is a slightly rounded wedge, with large, pointed ears and almond-shaped eyes. The coat has the same agouti-ticked fur and the same facial markings, but it is long, soft and silky, with horizontal tufts in the ears and tufts at their tips. The tail is plume-like and a generous ruff and breeches are desirable. The coat may be either ruddy or red in colour, as in the Abyssinian. The eyes are a rich gold or a deep green in colour.

RAGDOLL

This North American breed looks like the Birman in physique and coat. As originally bred and first accepted by one American association, its colour and markings resembled those of the Birman. Some other associations now also recognize both a bi-colour and a colourpoint version (that is, pat-

terned like the Siamese with dark paws). However, it is not its appearance that makes the Ragdoll so different from any other cat.

The first Ragdolls were a litter of kittens born to a cat that had been injured in an accident. The kittens were all extremely relaxed, even limp, like a ragdoll hanging over the arm— hence the name. They appeared to feel no pain and to have little sense of fear or awareness of danger. Such characteristics are unlikely to help them to protect themselves or to avoid injury. They are placid and calm cats, with extremely quiet voices. In the words of the original breeder, they are 'the closest one can get to a real live baby and still have an animal'. Whether this quality appeals will depend on your idea of what a cat should be like. Ragdolls require devoted attention from their owners, because they give little indication of any injury or illness. Owners will only find out if anything is wrong by carefully studying the cat's condition and behaviour, noting the smallest changes.

The original type of Ragdoll had the 'white gloves' of the Birman. This is the only variety recognized by the original breeder and one American association. Others have developed and gained acceptance from other associations for both the bi-coloured and colourpoint varieties (see page 90), and in them the original form is called the 'mitted'. Ragdolls tend to be large cats, with thick fur which forms a fluffy ruff and a long, full tail.

An accident could not have affected the genetic make-up of a parent's offspring, unless, perhaps, the parent was subjected to radiation, which does not appear here to have been the case. It must, therefore, be assumed that the Ragdoll was the result of a spontaneous mutation.

CYMRIC (LONG-HAIRED MANX)

This American cat is in all respects like the Manx (see page 65), except for the length of its fur. It was not created by crossing Manx with long-haired cats. Instead, it developed from a long-haired kitten, a mutant born in a litter of other short-haired Manx cats. Its parents and ancestors were pedigree Manx going back through several generations.

The Cymric (meaning Welsh), the name by which it is known in Canada, or Manx Long-hair, as it is known in the United States, has a medium length coat, which is softer than that of the normal Manx. The variety has the final vertebrae missing, the longer back legs and the same overall physical balance of the short-haired version. It is recognized in the same coat and eye colours.

BALINESE

This is another naturally occurring, long-haired mutation from a short-haired cat, in this case from the Siamese. It has the full Siamese-type head, body, tail and legs, the same vivid blue, oriental eyes, and the contrasting coat pattern of dark mask and points set against a lighter ground colour. It also has the lively personality and intelligence of the Siamese cat.

Except for the superficial similarity

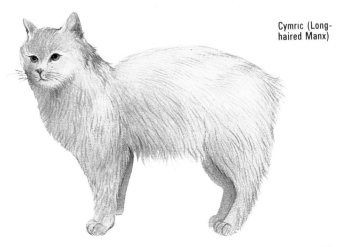

Cymric (Long-haired Manx)

of its coat pattern, this variety has nothing in common with the Colour-point or with the Birman. Siamese breeders were initially unhappy to find long-haired mutants in their litters. However, the soft, silky coats of these mutants were not like most of the rather rough and shaggy coats of some long-haired kittens that have been born occasionally to Siamese cats.

American breeders were the first to recognize their attractiveness. By breeding the naturally occurring long-haired mutants to each other, they produced a cat with luxuriantly long fur. There is now enthusiastic support for the Balinese in Britain, although there are not yet enough cats in the country for the variety to gain recognition. In North America, the Balinese is accepted in Seal Point, Blue Point, Chocolate Point and Lilac Point. It is possible that a wide range of colours will eventually gain recognition in Britain.

TURKISH CAT

Originally known in Britain as the Turkish Van, this natural variety comes from the area around Lake Van in Turkey. In type, it is closest to the Angora, which also comes from Turkey (see page 74).

The body of the Turkish Cat is long and sturdy, with medium-length legs and rounded feet. The head is wedge-shaped, but not so long as in the Siamese, although the nose is long. The ears are large, upright and set fairly close together. The eyes are round and light amber in colour. The

Lilac Point
Balinese

Seal Point
Balinese

Turkish Cat

fur is soft, long and silky. It has no woolly undercoat. The tail is full, the ears well-feathered, and there are tufts of fur between the toes. The coat is chalk white overall, with the exception of the medium-length, well-furnished tail, which is auburn, with faint, darker rings. There are also auburn markings on the face which extend from the base of the ears, but leave a white blaze between them, the ears themselves being white. The nose leather and paw pads are pink, as are the insides of the ears, and there are rims of pink skin around the eyes. Turkish cats of other colours can be seen in Sweden. These came from other provinces of Turkey.

Males, in particular, are sturdy and muscular, especially on the neck and shoulders. They are hardy cats. In their native countryside, they must endure snow for half the year. They have earned the nickname of 'Swimming Cats'. All cats can swim if they have to do so, although they cannot keep it up for long without exhaustion and, if unable to get ashore fairly quickly, they may soon be in difficulties. Turkish Cats really seem to enjoy being in water. They even like to be bathed, as well as swimming in shallow streams. If you bathe one, keep the water around their own blood temperature, 38°C (101°F). Unless it is a hot, sunny day, when the cat can shake itself and dry out naturally, you should dry it rapidly with a warm towel and not let it lie about with wet fur.

The first Turkish cats to arrive in Europe were a gift from Turkish friends to a British breeder who took them home. With others which she has since imported, she has gradually built up the breed. However, there are still few of these affectionate and intelligent cats in Britain and, because they tend to have small litters, they may remain difficult to obtain for some time. They are not yet established in North America.

FOREIGN SHORT-HAIRS

The Foreign Short-hairs are also sometimes known as 'orientals' and, originally, some of them did come from the East. However, the word 'Foreign' in the name of the group refers only to their type and not to their countries of origin. The most familiar and typical cats of this group are the Siamese and their derivatives, but the Foreign Short-hairs also include the Russian Blue, the Abyssinians, the Havana, the Burmese and the Korat. The Japanese Bobtail has been included in this group of cats, because it is closer to them in some ways than the other short-haired cats. The Rex and the Sphynx could also be placed in the Foreign group, because they are of foreign physical type. However, they have their origin in normal short-hair ancestry and so they have been described as part of the short-hair group (see pages 69-71).

In general Foreign Short-hairs have wedge-shaped heads, with large, pricked ears and slanting eyes, slim bodies on long legs, and a long, tapering tail. However, there are many small differences from breed to breed. The fur of Foreign Short-hairs presents no grooming problems. Brushing with a short-bristled brush or even hand grooming alone will give their coats a polished sheen. Regular grooming, however, is needed to remove moulted fur. This is especially important when cats shed their coats as the weather gets warmer, or for cats which spend most of their time indoors in warm homes.

Foreign Short-hairs are not usually solitary creatures. They like company, feline or human. If their owners are away from home all day, they are happier if there is another animal to share their lives. They tend to mature earlier than cats of the other groups and females often begin to 'call' when only six months old.

RUSSIAN BLUE

Russian Blues were at one time known as Archangel Blues. It is thought that sailors brought these cats back to Britain from the port of Archangel, in northern Russia. There was regular trade between Britain and Archangel from Elizabethan

Opposite: This Seal Point Siamese is typical of the lithe-bodied svelte-looking Foreign Short-hairs.

times, but these blue-coated cats do not appear to have attracted attention until about 1860.

The Archangel cat had a small, triangular head set upon a long, slender body. Its coat was thick, soft and silky. For hundreds of years, cats with blue coats were known as Maltese cats and sometimes as Spanish cats. This created some confusion as to their geographical origin. The foreign type cat was not clearly differentiated from the British Blue.

Not only was there cross-breeding, but both types also competed in the same classes at shows. Shortly before World War I, separate classes were first given to the two types. The Russian Blue was then known as the Blue Foreign, a name which stuck for many years.

Scandinavian enthusiasts for the variety mated their only available Russian Blue to a Siamese in 1944. This led other breeders to introduce Siamese blood and so produce an overall change in the type. From 1965 there was a move to re-establish the original form and the British standard was revised to reflect the original type of Russian Blue.

The modern form of the breed has a short, wedge-shaped head, with a straight nose, strong chin and prominent whisker pads. The almond-shaped eyes are vivid green and set well apart. The ears are large and pointed, wide at the base and set vertically on the head. The skin is thin and transparent, with little inside hair. The body is long and graceful,

with long legs and small, oval feet and a fairly long, tapering tail. The double coat is soft, silky and very thick. It is an even and clear blue throughout, with a distinct silvery sheen. The nose leather and paw pads are blue.

The British cat is still of a rather more foreign type than is preferred in North America, where the ears are not so pointed and are set lower on the head. Lighter shades are preferred in the coat and American descriptions specify silver-tipping of the guard hairs, slate grey nose leather, and paw pads of lavender pink or mauve.

ABYSSINIAN

The Abyssinian cat was first listed as a separate breed under that name in 1882. Its origin is a matter of conjecture. It has been claimed that it is a direct descendant of the cats of the Egyptian pharaohs and that it was brought to Britain from Ethiopia by soldiers returning from the Zulu wars in 1868. It has also been suggested that it is the result of a careful breeding programme by British breeders who wanted to produce a cat like the ancient type and who used tabbies which appeared with the agouti pattern of individually striped hairs which sometimes occurs in tabby lines. However it came about, the Abyssinian's coat does have similiarities with that of the African Wild Cat and its form closely resembles some of the cats depicted in ancient Egyptian paintings and sculptures.

This medium-sized cat has a firm and muscular build, but it is elegant and lithe. The body and the tapering tail are fairly long. The legs are slim, with small, oval feet. The head is broad and wedge-shaped, but gently contoured without flat planes. The muzzle is not pointed and is shaped by a shallow indentation on either side. There is a slight rise from the bridge of the nose to the forehead, a gentle rounding to the brow and a firm chin. The ears are large, broad-based, gently pointed and preferably tufted. The eyes are large and almond-shaped.

The Abyssinian coat is made up of short, fine fur, of which each hair is striped with two or three bands of colour. There should be no barring or stripes on the legs, chest or tail, though there should be a solid area of darker colour at the tail tip and up the back of the hind legs. There is a line of darker colour around the eyes and dark lines also extend from the corner of the eyes over the forehead. These and the eye outlines are set against lighter fur. Many Abyssinians have white patches around the lips and over the lower jaw. These are undesirable. If they extend on to the neck and undercarriage, they constitute a definite fault.

Two colours of Abyssinian are

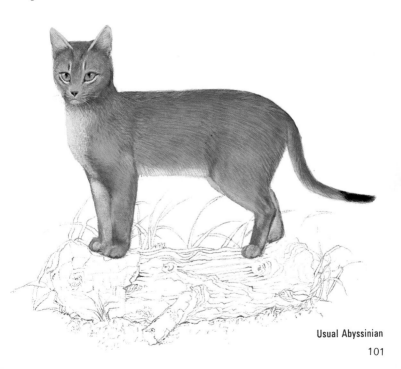

Usual Abyssinian

Blue
Abyssinian

Sorrel (Red)
Abyssinian

recognized in Britain and North America. A third is provisionally recognized in Britain.

USUAL ABYSSINIAN

The Usual, or Ruddy, Abyssinian is the original Abyssinian variety. The body colour is a rich golden-brown, ticked with black, and the base hair is a ruddy orange or rich apricot. The belly and inside of the legs harmonize with the base hair. If there is any shading down the spine, it is of a deeper colour. The tip of the tail and the solid colour on the hind legs are black. The paw pads are black and the nose leather brick red. The eyes may be amber, hazel or green, but they should be rich in colour. In North America they are described as greenish-gold or hazel.

SORREL (RED) ABYSSINIAN

The Red variety of the Abyssinian has a body colour of lustrous copper red,

which is ticked with chocolate. The base hair is deep apricot, as is the hair of the belly and inside of the legs. The tail tip, the back of the hind legs and any shading along the spine are chocolate. The nose leather and paw pads are pink. The eye colour is the same as for the Usual Abyssinian. Cream Abyssinians have also been bred in which all these colours are diluted but this variety has not yet been recognized.

BLUE ABYSSINIAN

Although not yet fully recognized, the Blue Abyssinian has a provisional standard which describes the base hair as pale cream or oatmeal with a body colour of blue-grey ticked with a deeper steel blue. The tail tip and the solid colour on the hind legs are also steel blue. The nose leather is dark pink and the paw pads are either mauve or blue. The eye colour is the same as for other Abyssinians.

SIAMESE

The Siamese does have a genuine connection with Siam, or Thailand as it is now called. Thailand, however, is not necessarily the country where the breed originated. The characteristic pattern of the coat has appeared occasionally as a mutation in many lands and it seems likely that the Siamese probably developed first even farther east. Despite the differences in length of fur and physical type, it has been suggested that the Siamese could be linked with the Birman (pages 90, 92), or even be a partly albino development from the Burmese (page 115), although the first cat known as a Burmese in North America was actually a hybrid Siamese! A German explorer came across a cat somewhat like a Siamese in the Caspian Sea region in 1794 and he published a picture of it. He said that it was born of a black mother and so it was perhaps just one of the mutations that occur from time to time.

Various tales are told of the way in which the Siamese cat was the guardian of Buddhist temples and of the palaces of Siamese kings. The kinked tail that was once common in the breed was said to have resulted from the zeal of a cat guarding a precious chalice. To do this, it twined its tail around the stem of the cup and, when it was relieved eventually of its charge, its tail was permanently twisted. Another story relates that the kink originated when a princess took off her rings to go bathing and slipped them over the tail of her cat, tying a knot in it to ensure that they did not fall off. When the poor cat's tail was untied, it failed to recover completely. It was said that the crossed eyes, which were also once a common feature of the breed, were gained by the cats concentrating hard on the prized objects that they were set to guard.

Siamese cats are certainly not the common cat of Thailand today and they seem never to have been so. They were court animals and this fact influenced their careful breeding. An antique scroll of verses and pictures, probably copied from an original produced in the Ayudha period, 400 years ago, shows a picture of the Siamese, which it called the Vichien Mas. It is said that the cats were never sold and they were given as presents only as a token of high honour, though it is possible that some were smuggled out.

The breed is said to have been introduced to Europe through a pair of cats given to the British Consul in Bangkok by the Thai court. He took them to England in 1884, but Siamese cats were actually known in Britain more than a decade earlier than that. However, these Siamese were very different from the breed we know today. They had roundish heads and heavy bodies, although they displayed the characteristic mask and points pattern.

The modern Siamese cat is extremely elegant and svelte. It is of medium size, with a long body, slim legs and dainty, oval feet, the hind legs being slightly longer than the front ones. The tail is long and thin and tapers to a point. The head is wedge-shaped, with a smooth outline both in profile and from the front. There may be a slight change in angle at the top of the nose, but otherwise it narrows in perfectly straight lines from large, wide-based, pointed ears to a fine muzzle, with a strong chin and a level bite. There should be no pinching in of the cheeks nor any roundness. The eyes are almond-shaped and placed at a slight angle to the nose. They should be a clear, deep blue, whatever the colour of the coat, except for those which are lilac-pointed or lilac-pointed tabby, when the British standard allows for eyes of lighter blue.

The Siamese pattern consists of

clearly defined areas of darker colour set off against a pale coat. These areas, or points, are restricted to the tail, legs, ears and mask, which spreads out across the face, covering the nose and mouth, the upper cheeks and the centre of the forehead. Lines of colour link the mask to the bottom of the ears. The fur along the spine may be a darker shade than the main part of the coat. It usually becomes progressively darker as the cat grows older. Elderly cats may have darker fur over much of the body, but the point pattern will remain clearly defined. In hot weather, or sometimes if a cat is unwell, brindling may develop within the darker coloured fur.

Siamese were once thought to be a rather delicate breed, but this is not true today, although they can sometimes prove bad invalids and give up the fight. As in all cats, a strain with a particular weakness may appear. For example, in recent years, a tendency to leukaemia has appeared in certain blood lines, but tests can now identify this and its perpetuation can be avoided. Unfortunately, as with dogs, the demand for extremely popular breeds of cat does sometimes lead to breeders using less than perfect animals.

Although not delicate, Siamese can certainly be demanding. They like attention and involvement. They are intelligent and resourceful. Skilful thieves and adept at getting their own way, they learn rapidly. There is an occasional dimwit, or are the apparent dimwits really the cleverest, giving a subtle performance to ensure that they get special attention? Siamese become extremely attached to their owners and, sometimes, to one person in particular. They can display a petulant jealousy if undue affection is shown to other animals or people! They are talkative, even argumentative, and many owners claim to be able to carry on comprehensible conversations with them.

It is important to establish good discipline when Siamese are young. They might otherwise develop into wilful cats that always manage to get their own way. Owners who have the patience to teach their cats to walk on a lead are more likely to have success with a Siamese than with most other breeds.

Seal Point Siamese

Females frequently reach sexual maturity early. Kittens have been known to begin 'calling' when only four months old. The call of a queen in season can be raucous and disturbing to those not used to it. Even the normal voice of the Siamese sounds harsh compared with that of many cats. Perhaps it is the voice that makes some people think of the Siamese as a spiteful, deceitful cat. Owners of Siamese would vehemently deny this, although they would admit that it is a breed that will assert its rights and use its cunning.

Siamese often bear large litters. The kittens are born with a fluffy, nearly white coat and no markings. Their eyes open earlier than most cats. The mask and points begin to appear faintly as they grow. The area around the nose is usually the first to darken. Kittens with a mixture of colours in their ancestry cannot always be positively placed in any particular colour variety until they are near weaning age. The pencilling that links the face mask to the ears may not develop until the cat is fully adult.

The Seal Point was the first variety of Siamese to be recognized. There are now a large number of colour varieties.

SEAL POINT SIAMESE

The body colour of an adult Seal Point Siamese is cream, shading into a pale, warm fawn on the back. It will be paler in kittens and, in most cats, there will be some darkening of the back with age. The mask, ears, legs, feet and tail are clearly defined in seal brown. This rich, dark brown is genetically black, being lightened slightly by the same genetic coding that controls the pointed pattern. No dark marks should occur anywhere else, although a number of cats have a dark blotch on the belly. Light 'spectacles' around the eyes or light patches on the feet would disqualify a cat from exhibition in a show, but these features are now rare. The nose leather and paw pads should match the points in colour, except in North America, where the paw pads may be pink.

BLUE POINT SIAMESE

The Blue Point was the second of the Siamese colours to be recognized. It was appearing regularly in both

105

British and American shows by the 1920s. The first was registered as long ago as 1894, before the standard for the Siamese was firmly established.

The cat's body colour is a glacial-white shading into blue on the back, but even there it is of a lighter tone than the points and mask which should be a clear blue, the ears being of even colour with the mask and limbs. The eyes are a clear, vivid blue. The nose leather is slate blue, as are the paw pads in Britain, but the paw pads are pink in North America.

CHOCOLATE POINT SIAMESE

The Chocolate Point, a further dilution of the Seal, was seen occasionally among the earliest Siamese. It was then often considered to be a poorly coloured Seal. However, it owes its colouring to a different gene. Chocolate Points were not officially recognized until 1950, at first in Britain and then in other countries. The body colour is ivory, shading, if at all, to the colour of the points. The points are the colour of milk chocolate. The

nose leather and paw pads match the points or, in North America, they are described as cinnamon pink and pink.

LILAC POINT SIAMESE
(FROST POINT SIAMESE)

In the United States, the Lilac Point Siamese was originally known as the Frost Point. Its colouring occurs when both parents carry recessive genes for both Chocolate and Blue. Lilac Points bred to Lilac will produce lilac kittens.

The body colour is off-white. The standard for British cats describes the shade as magnolia. In North America some associations ask for milk white or glacial-white. The mask and points are pinkish-grey according to the British standard, with nose leather and pads of faded lilac. In North America, the description is given as frost grey, with a pinkish tint, and the nose leather and pads are described as faded lilac. In North America the eyes should be deep or brilliant blue, but the British standard allows for a light, but not pale, vivid blue in this colour variety.

Chocolate Point Siamese

Lilac Point Siamese

RED POINT SIAMESE (RED COLORPOINT SHORT-HAIR)

The Red Point variety of the Siamese was first recognized in North America in 1956. Recognition came a decade later in Britain. This variety has a white coat, with shading to pale apricot being permitted on the back. The points are a bright reddish-gold according to the British standard,

Red Point Siamese

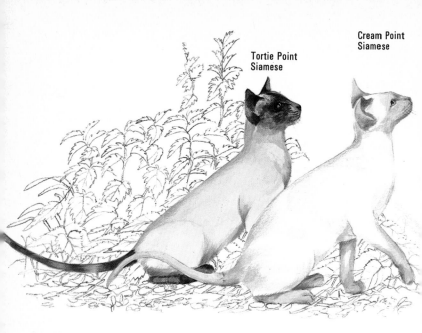

Tortie Point
Siamese

Cream Point
Siamese

with the legs and feet being reddish-gold to apricot. In North America the colour is described as deep red. The nose leather and paw pads are pink. The eyes are vivid blue.

Some American organizations refuse to recognize any colours other than Seal, Blue, Chocolate and Lilac as true Siamese. They call them Colorpoint Short-hairs (see page 110).

As in other red cats, the colour of the Red Point is sex-linked, which made the creation of the variety more difficult for breeders. The dilution factor, which makes the Seal Siamese appear dark brown rather than black, also weakens the red coloration. Further complication is added by the persistence of tabby markings in red-coloured cats.

TORTIE POINT SIAMESE (TORTIE COLORPOINT SHORT-HAIR)

This is a female-only variety. It can

be produced when a Seal Point is mated with a Red Point, or when a Tortie Point is mated with any other Siamese colour. The points are a bi-colour or tri-colour mixture of red and/or cream, with either seal, blue, chocolate or lilac. The body colour is the equivalent of whatever is appropriate to the incorporated colour. Feet, legs, tail, ears and mask should all be made up of mingled colours, as should the nose leather and paw pads. However, the distribution may be random and it does not have to follow a regular pattern.

American organizations, which do not recognize this colouring in the Siamese, class this variety as a Tortoiseshell Colorpoint Short-hair (see page 110).

CREAM POINT SIAMESE (CREAM COLORPOINT SHORT-HAIR)

The Cream Point Siamese, a further dilution of the Red Point, has a white body coat. If there is any shading, it is only of the palest cream. The points are a cool, clotted cream shade, warming towards apricot on the nose, ears and tail, but avoiding a hot shade. The nose leather and paw pads are pink. The eyes are a vivid blue. This is another variety which is grouped with the Colorpoint Short-hairs by those who do not class it as Siamese (see page 110). Cream Point Siamese almost always carry tabby markings. They are then indistinguishable from Cream Tabby Points.

TABBY POINT SIAMESE (LYNX POINT SIAMESE, OR TABBY COLORPOINT SHORT-HAIR)

The Tabby Point Siamese appeared in the early 1900s and again some 40 years later, when they were known as Silver Point Siamese. It was not until the 1960s, however, that they began to attract much attention. They had been variously called Shadow Points, Attabiys and Lynx Points, but it was as Tabby Points that they were recognized in Britain in 1966. In Australia, New Zealand and North America, they have retained the name Lynx Point, although some American associations class them as Colorpoint Short-hairs and do not accept them as Siamese (see page 110).

As is obvious from their name, they have the points and mask of the Siamese in the form of tabby markings. They may be in any of the recognized Siamese colours: Seal, Blue, Chocolate, Lilac, Red, Cream or Tortoiseshell. The body should be clear of markings. However, the Tabby Point, like other Siamese, develops darker marking on the back with age.

The body colour should be of the appropriate colour to match the colour of the points, as described for that particular colour Siamese. The legs have broken horizontal stripes of varying size, with the back of the hind legs of solid colour. The tail is marked with many clearly defined

Tabby Point Siamese

rings and ends in a solid-coloured tip. The mask has clearly defined stripes, especially around the eyes and nose and on the forehead, with distinct markings on the cheeks and darkly spotted whisker pads. The ears are solid-colour without stripes, but there is a pale smudge on the back of the ears, like the impression of a thumb. The nose leather and paw pads conform with the colours described for the Siamese of the colour of the markings, or they may be pink. The eyes are brilliant blue, with the lids either darkly ringed or toning with the points. Tortie-Tabby Points differ slightly in having mottled ears, but they should resemble the tabby pattern more strongly than the tortoiseshell.

COLORPOINT SHORT-HAIRS

This is the name given by some North American associations to the varieties which are known in Britain as the Red, Cream, Tabby (Lynx in America) and Tortie Point Siamese. These varieties are described above.

A Blue-Cream Point, Chocolate-Cream Point and a Lilac-Cream Point are also recognized. They are dilute forms of the Tortie Points, but they are otherwise similar to them.

The term Colorpoint Short-hairs should not be confused with the British Colourpoints, which Americans call Himalayans (see page 90). The different American and British spellings distinguish between the two types.

FOREIGN WHITE

The Foreign White is another form of Siamese, although it lacks the distinctive Siamese point pattern in its coat, which is completely white. The paw pads and nose leather are pink and the eyes are brilliant blue.

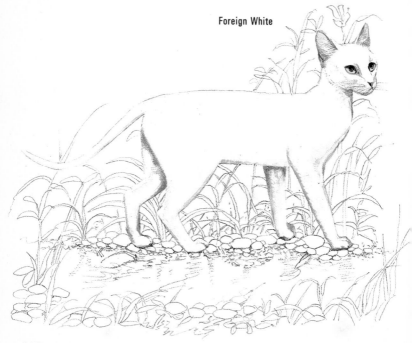

Foreign White

In this variety, the genetic factor which restricts the coloured fur of the Siamese to the mask and points is so dominant that it removes them altogether. The cat is not an albino and there is none of the pinkness about the eyes that is common to albinos of all species. When the breed was being created from Siamese in which the colour restriction was extreme, there were problems in that the deafness associated with blue-eyed white cats appeared. However, by careful selection in breeding, experts believe that inherently deaf strains have been eliminated.

In North America this variety would be grouped with other cats of Siamese type that are of one colour. These cats are called the Oriental Short-hairs (see page 113).

FOREIGN BLACK

The Foreign Black is another variety originating from the Seal Siamese. It is the opposite in development to the Foreign White, being a Siamese in which the restriction factor has become so recessive that it has ceased to be effective. Not only does the colour extend over the whole of the cat's coat, but the dilution effect, which creates the seal tone, has also been lost so that the cat has glossy black fur all over. The eyes are green. The paw pads and nose leather are black. The Foreign Black has the characteristics of the Siamese in every other way. This cat was recognized only recently in Britain. The corresponding breed in North America is the Ebony Oriental Short-hair.

FOREIGN LILAC

Lilac cats are produced when both parents carry the genes for both blue and chocolate and some examples of

Foreign Lilac

Foreign Black

a Siamese cat with a solid lilac coat appeared during the creation of the Havana. During the 1960s, breeders began to give attention to its development as a distinct type of Siamese, whose soft and glossy coat is frost grey with a pinkish tone. The nose leather and paw pads are pinkish. The eyes are vivid green. The corresponding breed in North America is the Lavender Oriental Short-hair. It is also sometimes known as the Foreign Lavender.

HAVANA (HAVANA BROWN)

The Havana is a Chocolate Siamese in which the dilution factor does not operate, leaving the glossy coat a rich, chestnut brown throughout, being slightly darker than the colour of the ancestral Chocolate. The whiskers and nose leather are the same colour as the coat, but the paw pads are pinkish-brown. The eyes are green, but oriental in shape and setting. The head, ears, body, legs and tail all follow the standard for the Siamese in shape and balance, at least in British and European cats.

Both Black Short-hairs and Russian Blues were mated with Chocolate Point Siamese in the early stages of the creation of this variety. At first they were given the name Havana, but this was changed to Chestnut Foreign Short-hair for a time. The name Havana was re-established in 1970.

Breeding Havana to Havana can lead to a loss in the foreign look. Crosses back to Chocolate Point Siamese have proved necessary to maintain it.

The first Havanas in North America came from Britain. However, the American strain, now called the Havana Brown, was not crossed back to Siamese and a different cat has resulted. It has a more rounded muzzle, round-tipped ears, a distinct stop level with the eyes, and a slight break behind the whiskers. Its eyes are dark green in colour and the nose leather is rosy in tone.

Havana

ORIENTAL SHORT-HAIRS

This is the name under which all the solid coloured Siamese cats are grouped by North American associations. This group does not include the Havana, which is less Siamese in type than it is in Britain and Europe, but it does include the equivalents of the British Foreign White (page 110), the Foreign Black, known as the Ebony in North America (page 111), and the Foreign Lilac, known as Lavender (page 111). In addition the group includes many other colours that are not recognized in Britain: Blue, Chestnut, Red, Cream, Silver,

Cameo, Ebony Smoke, Blue Smoke, Chestnut Smoke, Lavender Smoke and Cameo Smoke. Also recognized are both classic and mackerel tabby patterns of Ebony, Blue, Chestnut, Lavender, Red, Cream, Silver and Cameo and Tortoiseshell, Blue-Cream, Chestnut Tortie and Lavender Cream.

These cats have the physique of the Siamese, but their eye colour is green or amber, except for the White, which may have blue or green eyes. However, the White may not be odd-eyed. Oriental short-hairs tend to have softer voices than the Siamese.

113

Egyptian Maus
(Oriental Spotted Tabbies)

EGYPTIAN MAU (ORIENTAL SPOTTED TABBY)

This variety was produced in a conscious attempt to create a cat which would look like those in ancient Egyptian paintings and sculptures. Whereas the Abyssinian suggests the type and is similar to the African Wild Cat, the Egyptian Mau, as it was first generally known, is like those spotted cats seen in murals and on papyri.

The North American Mau line has a geographical link with Egypt because the cats are derived from animals which came from Cairo via Rome. Three were shown at a cat show in Rome in the mid-1950s. They were the first of the breed in North America, establishing two colour varieties : the Silver and the Bronze.

In Britain the Mau did not have its origin in imported cats but in tabby kittens of foreign type which ap-

peared during the breeding of the Tabby Point Siamese. Acknowledging its ancestry, its British name was changed to the Oriental Spotted Tabby when it received official recognition as a breed in 1978.

The British cat is of extreme foreign type, being in effect a spotted Siamese. It has striped limbs, a ringed tail and tabby markings on the head, which include a pattern on the forehead like that of a scarab beetle. This beetle features in Egyptian art and religion and often appears on the foreheads of cat figures. The eyes are green. The coat can be of any of the accepted tabby colours.

The American cat is of less foreign type. Although the eyes are oval and slightly slanting, fully oriental eyes are considered a fault. The body is slightly more cobby than in the Siamese and the head is a more rounded wedge. Several colours are now recognized by various associations.

SILVER MAU
The Silver has a pale silver ground colour and charcoal grey markings. The nose, lips and eyes are outlined in black. The nose leather is brick red and the paw pads are black, the black extending beyond the paws of the hind legs.

BRONZE MAU
The Bronze has a ground colour ranging from tawny-buff on the sides to dark bronze on the saddle and a creamy-ivory on the belly. The markings are in dark brown. The nose, lips and eyes are outlined in brown, with brick red nose leather and black or dark brown paw pads.

SMOKE MAU
The Smoke has a charcoal grey coat over a silver undercoat, with jet black markings. The nose, lips and eyes are outlined in black. The nose leather and paw pads are also black.

PEWTER MAU
Some associations also recognize a Pewter variety, which has a pale fawn ground colour. Each hair is banded with silver and beige with black tipping, lightening to cream and losing the ticking on the belly. Markings range from charcoal to dark brown. The nose, lips and eyes are outlined in dark brown. The nose leather is brick red and the paw pads are charcoal to dark brown. Whatever the colour of the coat, the eyes should be light green, like a gooseberry, although an amber cast is permitted.

BURMESE
The Burmese cat seems genuinely to be a cat of the Orient and the female from which the western breed was developed was taken to North America from India. It is thought to have been a hybrid between a Siamese and a cat with a dark coat and, in North America, it was mated with a Siamese.

However, the Burmese is now a distinctly different type of cat from the Siamese. It has neither the extreme type of the Oriental, nor the cobbiness of the British Short-hair. Its body is of medium length, with a build that is more heavy and muscular than its appearance suggests. The chest is strong and rounded and the back is straight. The tail is of medium length, tapering only slightly to a rounded tip. The head is slightly rounded on the top, with full, wide cheeks, and tapers to a short, blunt wedge. The ears have slightly rounded tips and a forward tilt. There is a distinct nose break and a strong lower jaw. The eyes are large with the top edge having an oriental slant, while the lower edge is rounded. The coat is short, fine and close-lying, with a satiny texture. It is particularly glossy. An even less Siamese look is required in North America than in Britain, with more rounded eyes. The feet should also be round, not oval as in the British standard.

Burmese do, however, share some of the personality of the Siamese. They are extremely affectionate, people-oriented and given to jealousy. They have a reputation for strong family feeling, the males being as attentive as females to their kittens. They are great wanderers and should not be given unlimited freedom.

Four separate colour varieties are recognized in North America and a much wider range is recognized in Britain. The coat should be an even colour, shading gently to a slightly lighter colour on the chest, belly and inside of the legs. The mask and ears may be a shade darker than the rest of the cat. The eyes are ideally golden-yellow, but any shade from chartreuse to amber is permitted.

Brown Burmese

Blue Burmese

Chocolate Burmese

BROWN BURMESE (SABLE BURMESE)

In Britain the Brown Burmese is described as a warm seal brown. Kittens and young cats may be lighter and even show tabby markings. The nose leather is a rich brown and the paw pads are brown.

In North America the brown variety is known as the Sable Burmese. Some associations recognize only this original colour in the Burmese.

BLUE BURMESE

The standard for the Blue Burmese in Britain asks for a soft, silver grey coat, with a distinct silver sheen on rounded areas, especially the ears, face and feet. The nose leather is very dark grey and the footpads are grey.

The American standard calls for a rich blue, with the same iridescent sheen. The nose leather and paw pads are blue-grey with a pinkish tinge.

CHOCOLATE BURMESE

The Chocolate Burmese is a British variety. The coat is a warm, milk chocolate colour, with chocolate brown nose leather and paw pads of brick pink, shading to chocolate.

LILAC BURMESE

Another British variety, the Lilac Burmese has a pale and delicate dove grey coat which has a slight pinkish tinge, giving a rather faded effect. The nose leather is lavender pink. The paw pads of kittens are shell pink, becoming lavender pink with age.

RED BURMESE

The adult in this British-recognized variety has a coat of light tangerine.

Red Burmese

Lilac Burmese

Tortie Burmese

Cream Burmese

The ears are distinctly darker than the back. Slight tabby markings are permissible on the face. The nose leather and paw pads are pink.

TORTIE BURMESE

The Tortie Burmese, with the usual tortoiseshell mixture of brown, cream and red, is recognized in Britain. The colour and markings, however, are not so important as the overall type. The nose leather and paw pads may be plain, or blotched brown and pink.

CREAM BURMESE

The Cream Burmese, another British variety, has a rich cream coat when adult and may show slight tabby markings on the face. The ears are very slightly darker than the colour of the back. The nose leather and the paw pads are pink.

CHAMPAGNE BURMESE

The Champagne Burmese is the North American variety closest to the Cream. The coat is a rich, warm honey beige shading, as described for all Burmese. The nose leather is a light, warm brown and the paw pads are a warm, pinkish colour.

PLATINUM BURMESE

This American variety is a pale silvery-grey, with slight fawn undertones according to the season. The nose leather and paw pads are lavender pink.

BLUE-CREAM BURMESE

The Blue-Cream Burmese is another British-recognized colour variety. The coat is a mixture of blue and cream with no obvious barring. The colour and markings are less important than the Burmese type. The nose leather and paw pads are plain, or blotched blue and pink.

TONKINESE

This relatively recent American hybrid breed was created by crossing the Siamese and the Burmese, between which there are greater differences in North America than in Europe.

The Tonkinese is a medium-sized, well-muscled cat. The head is a slightly rounded wedge, with a squarish muzzle and a rise from the bridge of the nose to the forehead. The ears are of medium size, with rounded tips, and they are tilted slightly forward. The feet are oval

Blue-cream Burmese

and the tail is tapering. The rich blue-green eyes are almond-shaped and slightly oriental.

The Tonkinese is now recognized in several colours. In all of them, the mask and points of the Siamese still show through as darker fur, but they do not have clearly defined edges. Instead, they merge gently into the body colour. The Natural Mink has a coat of warm brown, with dark chocolate to sable points. The Honey Mink has a more reddish-brown coat, with reddish points. The Tonkinese has also been produced in rich chocolate brown, champagne and blue-grey coats.

Tonkinese

Korat

KORAT

The Korat is a cat from Thailand, but it is very different from the cats we know as Siamese. The Korat has been known for centuries in its native country by the name Si-Sawat. *Sawat* means good fortune or prosperity and the people of the Korat plateau associate the cat with good luck and prize it highly.

It is a medium-sized cat. It is sturdy and muscular, with a medium-length tail that is heavy at the base and tapers to a rounded tip. The back is carried in a curve. Its legs are shorter than those of the Siamese. The face is heart-shaped, with a large, flat forehead and a strong but not sharply pointed muzzle. In profile there is a slight stop between the forehead and the nose, which has a slightly downward curve. Its ears are large and upright, with rounded tips. Its eyes are large and spaced widely apart. They are rounded when fully open, but have an oriental slant when closed or partly closed. The eyes change from blue in kittens to amber and then to a dazzling green-gold.

The coat is a silvery blue which is unlike that of any other breed. The silver tipping of the coat increases as the kitten matures, reaching its full strength at about two years old. An ancient Thai poem describes its fur as 'smooth with roots like clouds and tips like silver'. The nose leather, lips and paw pads are a dark blue or lavender, and the pads sometimes have a pinkish tinge.

Although Korats were occasionally seen outside Thailand, it was not until 1959 that a pair were taken to North America and the breed became established in the West. Korats were first recognized in North America in 1966. They are now an accepted breed in Britain, although not yet recognized for champion status.

JAPANESE BOBTAIL

The Japanese Bobtail is a variety that occurred naturally in Japan and owed nothing to artificial breeding. It has been known there for hundreds of years and is one of the types of cats which appears in Japanese paintings, sculptures and wood-block prints. The facade of the Gotokuji Temple in Tokyo is decorated with many pictures of these cats in a welcoming posture, with one paw raised. They are the *Maneki neko*, or the welcoming cats.

This cat does not fit into any of the basic physical types. Although more slender than the British or American Short-hairs, it does not have the full foreign look. The head is a triangle with gently curved sides. It has high cheek bones and a noticeable whisker break. The ears are large and upright, set more across the head than at the sides. The large eyes are oval and set at a slant. The Japanese Bobtail has long legs. The hind legs are longer than the front legs, but they are usually held bent when the cat is relaxed. This means that the body line remains level.

This breed's most distinctive feature is its tail, from which it gets its western name. At first sight the tail looks short and fluffy, like that of a rabbit. It often looks shorter than it is, because it is carried crookedly. There is a short straight section, only a few centimetres long, and there may be an angled section. The tail fur is longer and thicker than the rest of the coat, giving a pom-pom effect.

Japanese Bobtails can be produced in many colours. It is the *Mi-Ke*, the tortoiseshell pattern, however, which the Japanese associate with good luck. It is this cat which sets the pattern for the variety as accepted in North America. The coat is soft and silky and of medium length. It may be any of the combination of colours that make up the *Mi-Ke*: black, red and white; red and white; black and white; tortoiseshell or tortoiseshell and white; and solid coloured black, red or white. These cats have a reputation for intelligence and conversation, but their voices are chirrupy and gentle rather than strident as Siamese cats' voices sometimes can be.

Japanese Bobtails

GLOSSARY

agouti A coat pattern in which the individual hairs are banded with various colours, as in the Abyssinian cat.

albino An animal which lacks pigmentation in the hair and skin. The eyes of an albino are usually pinkish.

barring A form of tabby marking, a striped pattern. This is a fault when it occurs in self-coloured cats.

bi-colour A cat with a coat of two colours, one of which is white.

blaze A light, usually white marking running down from a cat's forehead to its nose.

blue In describing cat coats, a colour within the blue-grey range.

break *see* **stop.**

brindling Hairs of an incorrect colour scattered among those of the correct shade. This condition sometimes develops in hot weather in cats with otherwise good coats.

calling The making of repetitive and distinctive cries by a female cat which is in season. This unmistakable sound attracts the attention of local toms over a wide area and signals the female cat's readiness for mating.

chromosome The thread-like structure in the nucleus of animal cells which carries genetic material.

cobby Having a low-lying body on short legs.

dilution Variation in colour which produces a weaker shade in the coat.

dominant A characteristic which appears in the first generation of breeding, although it has been inherited from only one parent.

double coat Fur consisting of a thick, soft undercoat, which has another thick topcoat of long hairs over it, as in the Manx cat.

feral A once domesticated animal (or its descendants), now living wild.

frill The hairs around the head which form a frame to the face in long-haired cats. It is also called the ruff.

gene The part of a body cell which passes an hereditary characteristic from one generation to the next.

gloves White patches on the feet of some cats, as in the Birman.

haw ,The translucent third eyelid, or nictitating membrane.

heat A term used to describe the condition of a female cat when in season, that is, when the female is ready to accept a male for mating when she is said to be 'on heat'.

hot colour A too reddish shade in cream-coloured cats.

hybrid A type of cat which results from breeding one breed with another.

infertile Unable to breed.

laces White markings rising from the paw on the back of the rear legs, as in the Birman.

leather *see* **nose leather.**

litter (1) Kittens born to a female cat at the same time. (2) Clay granules, sand etc., used to fill a sanitary tray.

mask The darker colouring on the face which is seen in cats with a pattern of contrasting points, such as the Siamese.

mittens White patches on the front of the paws, as in the Ragdoll (see also **gloves**)

moggie A mongrel cat.

mongrel A cat of mixed, unknown parentage.

mutant An offspring which shows a genetic change from its parents. Mutants are sometimes a random occurrence. They can also result from exposure to X-ray or nuclear radiation.

neuter A castrated male or spayed female which is, therefore, unable to reproduce. It is also known as 'alter' or 'altered' cat in North America.

nictitating membrane The haw, or third eyelid.

nose leather The skin of the nose.

pads The fleshy cushions on the soles of the paws.

parti-colour A cat with a coat composed of two distinct colours, a bi-colour.

pedigree A genealogical table recording ancestry.

Persian A type of cat which is now officially known in Britain as a Long-hair.

points Darker coloured, contrasting areas on the head, ears, legs and tail, as in the Siamese.

pricked A term referring to ears that stand upright and high.

pure-bred With parentage and ancestry of the same variety.

rangy Long-limbed and long-bodied.

recessive A characteristic which is passed on from one generation to another, but which may not show in the first generation.

recognition Acceptance by the governing body of a cat association of the standard describing a new variety of cat.

ruff *see* **frill.**

rustiness A reddish-brown tinge in the coat of a black cat. It is sometimes caused when cats bask in the sun for long periods.

seal A rich dark brown, almost black colour, of which it is a slightly dilute form, as in the Siamese.

season The mating season, the time when a female cat is in oestrus and ready to accept a mate.

self or **self-colour** Of the same colour all over, without markings. It is also known as Solid or Solid-colour.

solid *see* **self.**

spaying The neutering of a female cat.

spraying Marking with urine.

standard or **standard of points** These are the characteristics required for a recognized variety of cat and the ideal description of the variety against which cats are judged in shows.

sterile (of cats) Infertile.

stop A break in the smooth line of the profile between the nose and the skull.

ticking Bands of colour on a single hair, see **agouti.**

tipping Contrasting colour on the tip of the hair, as in the Chinchilla.

tri-colour A cat whose coat is made up of three distinct colours.

undercoat Soft hairs which lie below the longer hair of cats with double coats.

Cats love warmth, whether curled up before a fire, stretched over a stove or basking in the sun.

INDEX

Note: Pages in **bold type** refer to the main entry on a cat. *Italic* numbers refer to illustrations.

Abyssinian 93-94, **100-102**, *101*, *102*
Aesop's *Fables* 32
African Wild Cat 9, 35, *35*, 36, 101, 114
Alice's Adventures in Wonderland 33
American Blue-Cream Long-hair **86**, *86*
American Short-hairs 59-64, 89; Bi-colour 63; Black **59**; Blue *59*, **60**; Blue-cream *63*, **64**; Calico 63-64, *63*; Cameo **60-61**; *61*; Chinchilla **60**, *61*; Dilute Calico *63*, **64**; Parti-colour 63; Red **60**, *60*; Shaded Silver **60**, *61*; Smoke **61-62**; Tabby *62*; Tortoiseshell 63; Tortoiseshell and White 63; White **59**
American Wire-hair **65**, *65*
Angora 39, **74**, *74*, 89
Apep 25, *25*
Archangel Blue *see* Russian Blue
Athens, carving *28-29*

Balinese **95-96**, *96*
Bast *24*, 26
Beresford Cat Club 39
Bi-colour American Short-hair 63
British Bi-coloured Short-hair **54-55**, *55*
Bi-colour Long-hair **85-86**, *85*
Birman 33-34, **90**, **92-93**, *92*, 103
Black American Short-hair **59**, 66
Black Long-hair (Black Persian) **75**, *75*
Black Short-hair **49**, *49*, 112
Blue Abyssinian **102**, *102*
Blue American Short-hair *59*, **60**
Blue Burmese *116*, **117**
Blue-cream American Short-hair *63*, **64**
Blue-cream Burmese **118**, *119*

Blue-cream Long-hair (Blue-cream Persian) **86-87**, *86*
Blue-cream Short-hair **55-56**, *56*
Blue Foreign 100
Blue Long-hair (Blue Persian) **76**, *76*
Blue Point Birman *92*, 93
Blue Point Siamese **105-106**, *105*
Blue Smoke Long-hair (Blue Smoke Persian) *83*, **84**
Blue Tabby American Short-hair 62, *62*
Blue Tabby Persian *80*, **81**
Bombay **66**, *66*, **68**
Breeding 41-45
British Blue **48**, *48*
British Blue-cream Long-hair **86**, *86*
British Short-hairs 47-59; Bi-coloured **54-55**, *55*; Black **49**, *49*; Blue-cream **55-56**, *56*; British Blue **48**, *48*; Chartreux **48**; Cream **51**, *51*; Smoke **58**, *58*; Spotted **53-54**, *54*; Tabby *46*, **51-52**, *53*; Tipped **58-59**, *58*; Tortoise-shell **56-57**, *56*; Tortoiseshell and White **57**, *57*; White **49-50**, *50*
Bronze Mau **115**
Brown Burmese *116*, **117**
Brown Tabby Long-hair (Brown Tabby Persian) **78**, *79*, 81
Brown Tabby Short-hair *52*, 53
Brueghel, Jan *36-37*
Burmese 66, 103, **115-118**, *116*, *117*, *118*

Calico American Short-hair **63-64**, *63*
Calico Persian **88**, *88*
Cameo American Short-hair **60-61**, *61*
Cameo Tabby American Short-hair *62*, 62
Cameo Tabby Persian *80*, **81**
Cat: Anatomy 10; Aggression *19*; Balance 14; Body language 18-19; Claws 21; Domestication 24, 35-36; Family 9; Foreign-Short-hairs 98-121; Fossil origins 8-9; Hearing 13; Hunting *18*, 19-21,

20, 21; Language 18; Learning 22-23; Long-haired cats 72-97; Retrieving 26, *27*; Short-haired cats 46-71; Sight 11-12; Smell 15-18; Tail 19; Teeth 21; Touch 15; Training 22-23; Washing 22-23, *23*
Cat Fancy 39, 45
Cat shows 39, 40, *40*
Champagne Burmese **118**
Chartreux 38, **48**
Cheetah *8*
Cheshire Cat 32, *33*
Chestnut Foreign Short-hair 112
Chinchilla American Short-hair **60**, *61*
Chinchilla Long-hair (Chinchilla Persian) **82-83**, *82*, 84
Chinese Desert Cat 35
Chocolate Burmese *116*, **117**
Chocolate Point Siamese **106**, *106*, 112
Chorozan 39
Christian Church (attitudes towards cats) 29, 30, 31, 33
Colorpoint Short-hairs 90, 108, 109, **110**
Colourpoints **90**, *91*
Cornish Rex **69-70**, *69*
Cream Abyssinian 102
Cream Burmese **118**, *118*
Cream Colorpoint Short-hair **108-109**, *108*
Cream Long-hair (Cream Persian) **77-78**, *78*
Cream Point Siamese **108-109**, *108*
Cream Short-hair **51**, *51*
Cream Tabby American Short-hair 62, *62*
Cream Tabby Persian *80*, **81**
Cymric **95**, *95*
Cyprus cats 38, 52

Devon Rex **70**, *70*
Dilute Calico American Short-hair *63*, **64**
Dilute Calico Persian **88**, *88*
Dinictis 8
Domestication 9, 24-26, 35-36
Doré, Gustave *34*

Ebony Oriental Short-hair 111
Egypt, ancient 24-27, *24*, *25*, *27*, *38*, 52, 114
Egyptian Mau **114-115**, *114*
European Short-hair *see* British Short-hair
European Wild Cat 9, 35, *35*
Exotic Short-hair **64-65**, *64*

Fédération Internationale Féline de l'Europe 39-40
Felidae 9
Felis bieti 35
Felis chaus 26, 35
Felis libyca 9, 26, 35
Felis silvestris 9, 35
Foreign Black **111**, *111*, 113
Foreign Lavender *see* Foreign Lilac
Foreign Lilac **111-112**, *111*, 113
Foreign Short-hairs 88-121; Abyssinian 100-102; Burmese 115-118; Colorpoint Short-hairs 110; Egyptian Mau 114-115; Foreign Black 111; Foreign Lilac 111-112; Foreign White 110-111; Havana 112; Japanese Bobtail 120-121; Korat 120; Oriental Short-hairs 113; Oriental Spotted Tabby 114-115; Russian Blue 99-100; Siamese 103-110; Tonkinese 118-119
Foreign White **110-111**, *110*, 113
Frost Point Siamese **106-107**, *107*

Genetics 41-45
Greece, ancient 28, *28-29*, 36

Hairless cats 70-71
Havana **112**, *112*
Himalayans **90**, *91*
Honey Mink 119

Japan, cats in 32-33
Japanese Bobtail 33, **120-121**, *121*
Jungle Cat 26, 35, 36

Kaffir Cat *see* African Wild Cat
Kliban 32
Korat **120**, *120*
Kuniyoshi 32

124

Lavender Oriental
Short-hair 112
Lilac Burmese **117,**
117
Lilac Point Balinese
96, *96*
Lilac Point Siamese
106-107, *107*
Long-hair (Persian)
74-88; Bi-colour
85-86, *85;* Black
75, *75;* Blue **76,**
77; Blue-cream
86-87, *86;* Blue
Smoke *83,* **84** ;
Calico **88,** *88;*
Chinchilla *72,* **82-
83,** *82;* Cream
77-78, *78;* Dilute
Calico **88,** *88;*
Parti-colour **85-86,**
85; Peke-faced
Persian **81-82,** *81;*
Red **76-77,** *77;*
Shaded Cameo *84,*
85 ; Shaded Silver
82, **83** ; Shell
Cameo **84-85,** *84;*
Smoke **83,** *83;*
Smoke Cameo *84,*
85 ; Tabby **78-81,**
79, 80; Tortoise-
shell **87,** *87;*
Tortoiseshell and
White **87-88,** *88;*
White **76,** *76;*
Long-haired Cats 72-
97; Angora 74;
Balinese 95-96;
Birman 90, 92-93;
Colourpoint 90,
91; Cymric 95;
Himalayan 90,
91; Long-haired
Manx 95; Long-
hair (Persian)
74-88; Maine
Coon Cat 88-89;
Ragdoll 94-95;
Somali 93-94;
Turkish Cat 96-97
Long-haired Manx
see Cymric
Lynx Point Siamese
109-110, *109*

Maine Coon Cat
88-89, *89*
Manx **65-66,** *67,* 95
Manx Long-hair *see*
Cymric
Matagot 31, *34*
Miacis 8
Mutations 41

National Cat Club 39
Natural Mink 119

Oriental Short-hairs
111, **113,** *113*
Oriental Spotted
Tabby **114-115,**
114

Parti-colour
American Short-
hair 63
Parti-coloured
Persian **85-86,** *85*
Peke-faced Persian
81-82, *81*
Persians, see Long-
hairs
Pewter Mau **115**
Platinum Burmese
118
Polydactylism 50
Puma *9*
Puss in Boots 31, *34*

Ra 25, *25,* 26
Ragdoll **94-95,** *94*
Red Abyssinian *see*
Sorrel Abyssinian
Red American Short-
hair **60,** *60*
Red Burmese
117-118, *117*
Red Colourpoint
Short-hair
107-108, *107*
Red Long-hair (Red
Persian) **76-77,** *77*
Red Point Siamese
107-108, *107*
Red Somali *93*
Red Tabby Long-hair
(Red Tabby
Persian) *79,* **81**
Red Tabby Short-hair
52, *53*
Rex **69-70,** *69, 70,* 99
Ruddy Somali *93*
Russian Blue
99-100, *100, 112*
Rusty-spotted Cat *9*

Sable Burmese *116,*
117
Sabre-toothed tiger
8, 8-9
Scottish Fold **68-69,**
68
Seal Point Balinese
96, *96*
Seal Point Siamese
98, 104, **105**
Seal Point Birman
92, 93

Shaded Cameo
American Short-
hair *61*
Shaded Cameo
Persian *84,* **85**
Shaded Silver
American Short-
hair **60,** *61*
Shaded Silver Persian
82, **83**
Shell Cameo
American Short-
hair *61*
Shell Cameo Persian
84-85, *84*
Short-haired cats
46-71; American
Short-hairs 59-64;
American Wire-hair
65; Bombay 66, 68;
British Short-hairs
47-59; Exotic
Short-hair 64-65;
Manx 65-67; Rex
69-70; Scottish
Fold 68-69;
Sphynx 70-71
Siamese 22, 90, 95,
98, **103-110,** *104,
105, 106, 107,
108, 109,* 110, 111,
112, 113, 114, 115,
118, 119
Siberian Tiger *9*
Silver Mau **115**
Silver Persian 82
Silver Tabby Long-
hair (Silver Tabby
Persian) **78,** *79*
Silver Tabby Short-
hair *46,* **52,** *53*
Si-Rex 70
Smilodon 8
Smoke American
Short-hair **61-62**
Smoke Cameo
American Short-
hair *61*
Smoke Cameo
Persian *84,* **85**
Smoke Long-hair
(Smoke Persian)
83, *83*
Smoke Mau **115**
Smoke Short-hair **58,**
58
Somali **93-94,** *93*
Sorrel Abyssinian
102, *102*
Sphynx **70-71,** *71,*
99
Spotted Short-hair
47, **53-54,** *54*
Sumxu 39

'Swimming cats' 97

Tabby American
Short-hair **62,** *62*
Tabby Colorpoint
Short-hair
109-110, *109*
Tabby Long-hair
(Tabby Persian)
78-81, *79, 80*
Tabby Point Siamese
109-110, *109,* 114
Tabby Short-hair *46,*
51-53, *53*
Tenniel, Sir John *33*
Thebes (painting) *26*
Tiger *8*
Tipped Short-hair
58-59, *58*
Tonkinese **118-119,**
119
Tortie Burmese **118,**
118
Tortie Colorpoint
Short-hair **108,**
108
Tortie Point Siamese
108, *108*
Tortoiseshell
American Short-
hair *63*
Tortoiseshell and
White Long-hair
(Tortoiseshell and
White Persian)
87-88, *88*
Tortoiseshell and
White American
Short-hair *63*
Tortoiseshell and
White Short-hair
(British) **57,** *57,* 69
Tortoiseshell Long-
hair (Tortoiseshell
Persian) **87,** *87*
Tortoiseshell Short-
hair **56-57,** *56*
Turkish Cat **96-97,** *97*

Usual Abyssinian
101, **102**

Vibrissae 15, *15*

White American
Short-hair **59**
White Long-hair
(White Persian)
76, *76*
White Short-hair
49-50, *50*
Witchcraft 29-30, *30,*
49

The author and publishers wish to thank the following for their kind help in supplying
photographs:

*Cover: Sally Anne Thompson. Title: Zefa. Contents: Ann Cumbers. Pages 24, 25, 27
& 38 Peter Clayton. Page 28/9 Ekdotike Athenon. Page 33 Mary Evans. Page 122/3
Keith Lye. Pages 30 & 34 Mansell. Pages 36/7 National Gallery. Pages 42, 46, 72 &
98 Sally Anne Thompson.*

Picture Research: Penny Warn.